I Wrote This Book in Lieu of Dying

Written by Audra Almond-Harvey
Edited by Merry MacIvor & Audra Almond-Harvey

REPRINTS: "I Mark Time With Observational Statements" originally published in Calliope Magazine, January 2015 and published here with permission. "Haunted By My Own Ghost" debuted as a live reading during *Haunted*, a Southern Gothic site-responsive immersive performance and installation. "Ghosts In The Night" debuted in 2016 during *Mundane Morose Meanderings*, performed in Nashville with frequent collaborator Tavius Marshall at the Kindling Arts Festival. "Ecclesiastes," "True Form," "Closets," and "To Be Free" all debuted in gallery during the author's solo gallery show, *Mostly Naked*, at abrasiveMedia in Nashville, TN in 2015. A work-in-progress of "A Letter To My Grandmothers Named Marie" debuted as a live reading in 2023 during *Invisible Ink*, a solo performance by the author during the Kindling Arts Festival in Nashville, TN.

For information, address the publisher at **info@abrasiveink.com**

ISBN 979-8-218-31460-6

for all my loves

This book would not be possible without the support of countless family and friends who have encouraged, cajoled, nagged, bullied, humored, and dragged me all the way to this finish line.

TABLE OF CONTENTS

IN WHICH I AM CAUGHT MONOLOGUING[1]

I have chosen what is perhaps an odd method for telling you who I am and what I have lived. My goal is not to recount events in chronological order. Instead, I describe my shifts in worldview and self-identity through seasons of metamorphosis.

Do you need to know that my father was born in 1945 and died on September 11, 1991, or is it enough to know that he died at home, and I still remember the smell of life leaving him? Would it help you to hear anecdotes of my interactions with teachers, or is it enough to know that I have learned many things and changed my mind several times based on new information?

As a teacher and leader, the characteristic I prize most in those with whom I work is independence of thought. I could tell you what to think, or even fully define what I think, but I do not prefer either option.

How do we even outline what we know about our memories? I might remember the same event in twelve different ways due to my evolving perspectives without changing the facts of what happened.

In an era of fake news, it is the role of some to teach an objective understanding of the differences between truth and untruth. However, the role that I have chosen is to convey that though most everything we remember is subjective—because that is just how brains do their thing— in the context of personal growth and an understanding of self, I believe the most honest retelling you can give is the one in which you are no greater or lesser than you truly are.

This work explores the impact of trauma through an invented literary

---

[1] The consistency of my monologuing tendencies is why I am either a terrible supervillain, or the best supervillain, depending on whom you ask.

format which I have termed "a poetic concept album inspired by many forms of storytelling, containing not a single note of music therein." While I disclosed most of the more horrific stories obliquely[2], there are some that I laid bare upon the page. If you have also experienced many generational, familial, and personal traumas, please know that I care far more about your mental health than I do about my readership numbers, and I will not be offended if this is not a work for you now.

I have often been asked, "Were you being sincere, or sarcastic?" in relation to words I have uttered. The answer has most always been "Yes." This is one of my child's favorite things about me.[3] Please keep this truth in mind as you read.

This book is about identity. In a story not uncommon in the southeastern region of the United States, many of my indigenous ancestors hid after the Indian Removal Act of 1830. The French and Spanish colonizers had taken my grandmothers' language, enslaved their bodies, erased their proper names in the baptismal pools, and gave them all the name "Marie."

Though I have cousins who walked the Trail of Tears, my direct Native ancestors hid in the backwater regions of Louisiana. As we are also Black through both enslaved people and free people of color, complex layers were added to our concealment during the Jim Crow era. Our people experienced a diaspora throughout the 1900s but never forgot our origins. Unified by the fear of being made known and the shame of being a hidden people, many of our stories and customs were passed down as family traditions or religious oddities. Some of us experienced a great deal of pressure assimilate and "pass;"[4] some of us never had the complexion to allow for that option. These patterns were reinforced in me, as they were in many of us, through experiences of personal trauma.

---

[2] I must admit to enjoying the torture of an occasional metaphor.

[3] This is an example of a statement that is both sincere, and sarcastic.

[4] The issue of who can and should "pass" as white is and has always been murky. Speaking specifically to the colonial history of Louisiana, there were a variety of racial definitions that could apply to a person depending on which power was in charge at the time. Thus, one individual could be racialized differently over the course of their lives. I will only be addressing the issue of passing from my personal experience and what I have learned of my family. I do not claim to speak on behalf of anyone besides myself.

The two generations before me led a movement to return, understand who we are, and proudly claim the heritages our grandmothers did much to protect. One of my elders once told me that my only responsibilities now are to come home and stop hiding. This is frankly terrifying and goes against every inborn and learned instinct I have. This book is my next step out of the shadows.

While you may be most familiar with conversations about identity from an individual perspective, much of the work I do while exploring my identity involves embracing the impact of my varying relationships with my ancestors; I believe that this work is the starting place to find my context. With some of my ancestors, I carefully note their choices and do my best to continue their work. With others, I try to recognize how they have taught me what I do and do not want to do in my own life. And with still others, the only rational and moral relationship I can have with them is one of defiance.

We are all familiar with the standard hero's journey, yes?[5] That is not my story at all.

I may not tell this story in order. I address many players in this loosely woven plot, rarely by name. I may say to you I believe something and then immediately contradict myself. I might hide my meaning in obscure references or bluntly lay it out on the page. I might present myself through sincerity or dry wit or overwhelming twee-ness or self-disparaging behavior or science fiction references. I poke fun at myself as often as I share deep feelings. I may start a thought, interrupt myself, and go in entirely different directions. I will not lie to you, even when a lie might make you like me more. I have done my best to present my ways of thinking as they were and are, without attempting to prove any rightness, for if I have learned anything, it is how often I have been wrong.

---

[5] Hero sets out on a quest, faces many challenges, has an inspirational chat with some form of Magic™ individual (a guru, a monk, a Vulcan, a wise old man of indeterminate origin with a bald head and/or long beard, an elf, a witch, a Black woman who also bakes or bartends), realizes the meaning inherent in the struggle of the journey, and then triumphantly accomplishes the quest with greater understanding of why they set out on the trip in the first place.

I have prayed two prayers that I know were fully honest. The first, prayed when I was four, was that I would have the wisdom of Solomon.[6] At the age of nineteen, the second was to tell God to fuck[7] off (but that if they wanted to prove their realness to me, they could).

I do not know if I have attained wisdom, though I have written about the many kinds of fools I have been. I have few proofs for anything, yet the faith I do hold provokes me profoundly and often.

In October 2015, my doctor told me she was not sure they would find out what was wrong with my health in time to help me and that I should get my things in order. So, I went online and downloaded a template for a will and an end-of-life-care plan, and then I went back to the meetings I had scheduled for that day. I did not have time to feel anything about it, so I rescheduled the Feelings About Impending Mortality for another time. I am still working through those feelings. I am also still kicking several years later[8], and I apparently had time to write a whole book of poetic prose.[9]

You can read this book forwards, backward, whilst drinking tea, in almost any setting, and before bed. You can write in this book (in fact, there are some blank pages for you to use however you wish). You can burn it, should your feelings about it be so strong as to require immolation. You can forget it on your bookshelf to collect dust. Love it, hate it, feel generally apathetic toward it; the way you honestly respond to this book is the response I want you to have.

Whatever you think of the words that follow, if you take anything away, I hope it is this: Regardless of life's inherent meanings or the lack thereof, it is the perfect time to tell your stories. *Now* is the only time I am confident we still have.

---

[6]   I was specific in my directions to God that I wanted to skip the whole being-a-king-with-hundreds-of-wives part.

[7]   This is one of only two instances of the word *fuck* in this book, so do not let this turn you off from reading further. Drat! Just kidding, one of *three* instances now.

[8]   Or, perhaps I am writing this from beyond the grave, and you are part of my purgatory...

[9]   As well as free-form prose poetry and other short-form non-fiction and philosophical works.

Many have used the analogy of a beautiful butterfly emerging from its cocoon to relate stories of personal transformation; I have portrayed a somewhat unsentimental view of this oft-romanticized concept.

You see, it is not real pretty. To begin the total transformation[10] of being, a caterpillar enters the process by transforming its body into goo through the excretion of enzymes. These enzymes dissolve the caterpillar's muscles into almost formless material, with some bits of organs suspended within the broth like a chunky stew, held together in a chrysalis form.[11] How does this soup become a winged creature in a manner of days? All-purpose cells called "imaginal discs" will eventually become legs, wings, antennae, compound eyes, and exoskeleton. But for a moment what was a caterpillar seems to have more in common with Newtonian fluids than it does with a moth.

I see parallels between this process and the ancient philosophies of the soul's metamorphosis. For example, in European Alchemic traditions, the ultimate great work[12] was not merely to transform lead to gold but to alter the human soul itself. The magnificent change of physical materials was a side effect of the end purpose: the alchemist resolving the duality of human and divine in her own person.

I do not know if I have a great work in me. I am not genuinely seeking enlightenment, nor do I strive for supernatural powers. I seek meaning and purpose for myself in the mundane, profound, and absurd experiences. I do not know what I will look like on the other side of this process—somehow, I doubt I will fly—but perhaps I will attain a measure of wisdom. Despite my ignorance, I believe the transformation is both inevitable and invaluable.

---

[10]   Or holometabolism.

[11]   Butterflies do not use cocoons. Only some species of moths weave cocoons. I realize some of you probably don't believe me, so feel free to go look that up now. Once you experience your crisis of belief and return to these words, you will have lived through an internal conflict of the like that has been the hallmark of my life. (The falsehoods taught in the form of childrens' illustrations are often the hardest to release.)

[12]   "Magnum Opus."

And so, like the caterpillar, I will begin here: First, I must digest myself.

Time may not flow in a linear fashion.

I would pour myself a beverage if I were you—

this could take a while.

VIGNETTES OF A DEAD MAN

YESTERDAY

I learned a lot from my father.

That's a loaded statement, for sure. But for now, let us start here: My father was a preacher. Each Sunday I sat in the pew and drew shapes with my fingers in the velour fabric covering the hard cushions, and I listened.

I noted his cadence, his rhythm. I observed the manner in which he drew his audiences into his stories, how he held them captive with his well-knit phrases.

Most importantly, I noted his pauses. The silence that he would allow to stretch on, long enough that my ears would collect each cough and shuffle and creak and sigh. I heard the wind, borne from the wrists of the parishioners waving paper fans to lighten the weight of the heat.

The silence could stretch out long enough that I would wonder if he lost his thoughts, until he gazed out to the pews and lay his subsequent words upon us, the heavy calm that ensued from his phrasing chafing me like a wool blanket on a summer night.

Take one breath, and two, and another
And hold it
Exhale

The silence around you has tones, flavors, textures.

Note the pauses.

HUES

I used to hold my arm next to yours,
comparing the hues of our skin and
noting that yours was so much
darker than mine.

I remember an ache that I could not name
then, but now know to be the desire to
be more like you so that you would have
someone who understood the
world as you saw it.

(We who see do so through our own eyes, the world illuminated by the
light reflecting off our own faces.)

I could not see your world as you did.

COMPOSE

There was this one day when the wind whipped around my bones.
The cloudburst penetrated until I was soaked through and my shoes
squished. I saw you splash in the puddles. We glanced across the terrain,
and for a moment, I could see through the drops of water as the putrid
haze was washed from the air. I walked lightly on the water, its surface
a pebbled glass. A sigh sounded from the wind as it finished the gale.
I blinked and opened my eyes again to find you still there. The shards
from the storm soaked deep, but there was no bleeding. The day was
warm again, the silence receding. The moment seemed an apparition,
but I wasn't dreaming.

PORTRAIT OF A YOUNG MAN

Tall, so tall that when I sat on his shoulders I got dizzy as I looked at the passing ground below; thin, with what my mother termed piano-wire muscles. Stronger than his form suggested. He stretched his hand toward mine as I climbed out of the car—I had to jump to catch it on the upswing—and then we dashed across the street. Well, he ambled; I ran on short legs, sometimes just clutching his hand with both of mine, feet skimming the ground, never quite finding purchase.

His eyes set firmly into a broad brow, face angled down, cut by sharp cheek bones, bound by a narrow chin. Course hair, beginning to gray but still so thick. Skin a dark sable in the summer and high yellow in the winter… never as pale as mine. His face told a complex story: of multiple tribes, of slaves and masters, of freeborn, and of the immigrants who wove through all those tales.

Mouth pursed as he scanned the street, as we headed with purpose to the ice cream shop where we would choose our flavors and then dissect all of existence (or as much as my vocabulary allowed me to comprehend) as our cones became soggy and melded with their bright paper wrappings.

I recall his voice was dark and booming and high and thin and loud and brash and quiet and reserved and silent, by turns. In this moment, I remember it was sharp and precise as he outlined his relation to the small, pudgy, pale-skinned child sitting across from him to the shop owner who had dared interrupt such hallowed proceedings with a crude question.

Now we're standing, though I have to hurry as he is already out the door, shoulders set pinched in his back, hands clenched, so I grab onto his wrist with all of my might in hopes of keeping up. Now he's slowing down, turning to me, sitting on the steps leading up to the empty storefront next door. A car whizzes past, a mosquito bites. It was late afternoon.

He grabs my attention with his hands, pulling my face toward him. I wait, breathing shallowly. This much silence before beginning means his words are carefully considered. He tells me we're moving to that long, hot, dry state after Texas and before Kansas, and I think for a bit, chewing my bottom lip, and I hesitantly ask if they have ice cream there, as all I remember of this place is that one dirty truck stop, and I know they don't have ice cream, and he laughs with a sharp, barking guffaw before bowing his head to take a deep breath, and then he looks up again to stare me down and asks if I have any more questions. So I ask, and he answers that it's dry and hot, and the wind blows fierce, and there aren't any swamps, and sometimes there are tornadoes, and there are lengthy times when it stops raining, and he doesn't really know what they eat, but it snows more than here, and we can make the biggest snowman, as tall as he.

"Taller?" I ask.

"Perhaps, if you sit on my shoulders."

There was a deep ache in my belly that told me that it would be forever until I felt at home again. He tells me that there are more Indians there, and perhaps we could visit the reservation where our people went when they got to Oklahoma. And I smiled at that but knew he was lying.

The winter after we arrived, it did snow, and I sat on his shoulders to finish the crown of the snowman's head. And I insisted on big ears because my father's ears protruded just so, and he laughed as he spoke of the kite we would build in the spring.

The winds did come in the spring, stronger gales than any I had known outside that one time the rain had blown sideways and the streets flooded. Our springtime kites were carefully made, and we were confident they would easily fly in such strong breezes. But they kept falling to the ground, no matter how hard and fast I ran as he threw my kite into the air.

That year, I learned in school that Oklahoma was "the land of the red man." I jumped from the home-bound bus in my hurry to rush inside to tell my mother that we were in the land of my father's people, and that meant it was his land, we belonged to this land, and we were finally home, even though I was sad to leave the swampy plains for the red clay. She gave me a look I had never before seen on her face, and that's the day I learned what the term "Indian giver" truly means.

That night, they yelled at each other in their bedroom while I hid under the rickety table near my bed, small hands covering my ears.

We never had another snowman and we gave up on kites so all that was left was to sit in the evenings on our couch and watch nature documentaries on PBS or old Westerns or Star Trek once in awhile. We would sit with some distance between us until he asked me to get up to turn off the television and then get ready for bed.

Later on, after I knew why the furrows in his brows were deepening, and after I knew what was growing in his belly, I thought it was fitting that he be buried there, in that red clay, not too far from the one tree on the wide plain swept clean by the wind, and the hands of death and time, though I couldn't tell you why.

The other day I looked in the mirror and I lost my breath for a second, because I saw him. He's in my eyes, and my brow, my chin. Though everyone has always said I look more like his sisters, I can see our resemblance clearly, now. I leaned close to the mirror, counted my gray hairs, and then turned off the light. I am the age he was when I was born.

The dirt is the proper color in Tennessee, that I can tell you. The tea is all wrong and almost nobody makes cornbread quite right, but I do what I can.

My daughter has the palest yellow skin. She has her father's brows but her face is structured after my pattern. I am teaching her how to make gumbo and to tell true stories. At night, we watch Star Trek. We've never gone kite flying, but when it snows, we make hot chocolate with marshmallows and eat ice cream. She occasionally obliges when I want to roll the snow into firmly packed rounds and stack them tall. She is a teenager now, so we'll see how that lasts.

She once asked me, when she was little, if I thought my father would have become such an angry and bitter man if he had known he was loved and if he had received more hugs than he did scary stories. I told him that probably would've made a difference. And then she asked if I thought my father was a bad man. I said he was a sad man, and an afraid man, and I don't think very many people are really villains, they're just stuck in the role because that's what society dictated, but society rarely dictates directions for how to escape. She didn't understand what I said then, I don't think.

She hugs me often still, though she's grown.

We have never seen the reservations.

Every year, on the anniversary of my father's death, I sing the song he taught me. The notes go just so.

I have to tell you all this because the pictures of my father have faded, as though they all were processed with a filter in the places you wish would never fade because those are the parts you just can't think of quite right. All his siblings have passed, so there's no one left to tell me who I come from except my mother, and it's been years since she remembered. But she is happy to live in the South again, and I thought the other day that it would be fitting to bury her here when it's her time, though I can't tell you why that is.

GHOSTS IN THE NIGHT

Here is my story, true as it is. Two people left:
one tangible, one a ghost. It was an old tale—
so predictable, so trite. Preacher-man,
he had a daughter.

But another tale—so offensive, such a blight.
That colored man's child is dirt in the water.

I remember, see? That's what they told me
wouldn't happen. I was supposed to sit,
still and quiet-like, and all would
be fine. I wouldn't even
remember.

But I do, and so I must have done something all wrong.

See, I remember their figures, tall, round
in the middle like biscuits, pale and
battered at the edges.

I remember where they stood, as they locked eyes
with my daddy, he in his pulpit,
they in their pew.

I remember one of them tugged at the waist of
his jeans and turned to the other, and then
looked right at me.

I lost some time—I don't know how we got in
the back room. I didn't see the moment that

we was gathered, me and my mama,
and her mama, and my daddy, all
tall and clothed in the grey suit
that reminded me of
a sky before
the rain.

But then, there we were, standing so
still, even as I felt the air pull thin
all around me. The time just
stopped right there, and
rushed past me
with a roar, in ways
together-like, as
I saw monsters
so cruel you'd
never think
they are
real.

Except, maybe, they were just a common kind
of cruel. I don't have so many answers,
except that one. As you see, the world
is still fraying on its seams. It's
not a new story, I
guess, but it's true
just the same.

This is how it was.

I didn't know their names. I only knew their
vests and jeans and belts and the dark
shiny thing sitting all pressed up to
one of them's side, like me
against my mama

when the night
 was too
 full.

They told my daddy that if I was still and
 quiet, everything would be fine, and
 we could all go home, and no one
 would be taken outside to be
 shot like a dog.

They said I wouldn't remember, but I do,
 so I must have done something
 all wrong.

Their specters followed me, you see, every which
 place we drifted to and landed in. They were
 the ghosts in the night, the monsters
 under my bed, the reason
 I wouldn't open my
 closet in the
 dark.

It was some years before I realized that they
 couldn't follow me no more, not them
 ghosts, they hadn't the right. But I
 still feel what it meant to be small
 and foolish and young and all
 held up in my father's arms,
 afraid, and so
 still. As quiet as
 I could be.

I know I must have done something wrong—
 I kept my tongue as well as I could, but
 all that effort must have been for

naught. I know I failed him.
My daddy never
quite left that
place.

The monsters trapped his ghost. Oh,
he did die a slow death, miles and
miles away from that back room.
But I don't think I ever saw
him stand so proud
ever again. Not before
he was gone.

I remember one night. I was sitting by the
bookshelf next to his bed, the long lines
of tomes stretching as tall and dark as
columns in a temple, like the pictures
in his books, holding up a high
ceiling beyond my sight, as I was
watching him fade in a croupy
dissolution, and wishing
that lightning would
strike so quick, and
so precise, that
he could end,
all at once,
but not
alone.

I didn't know that wish was right evil—
not then. But you see I was still
young, and a bit foolish, and
thought I knew just the
way that things
should be.

But I'll tell you this, it's as
 true as truth can be in this world.
 His ghost might still be there, in
 that back room, 'cause that's the
 last place I saw him stand tall.
 He might still be waiting,
 still, all grey and dark,
 and quiet-like, as
 quiet as can be,
 just in case
 you won't
 remember.

I wonder if anyone ever escapes. There it is. It's
 not a good ending, but it's a true one. That's
 all I got right now. Maybe I'll have
 answers later, on that inevitable
 day when I, too, find death's
 slow crawl at its close. Or
 perhaps I will be felled
 in a hair-trigger
 completion.

It's an old story, predictable and trite.
 Preacher-man's daughter tried
 to do right.

Two people left—just you and me.
 Perhaps I am the ghost.

Sometimes, when it's so late, and yet I
 cannot grasp tightly enough onto my
 slumber, I think of those long,
 warm days, the sun high
 in the sky, the air

pressing close
against my
skin.

I remember putting on my best dress and
my Sunday shoes to wade in the water.
And when the sun fell heavy into
the ground for the night, I
stood right there,
still and
quiet.

And I waited, breath drawn.

WHAT IS REAL

Gotta keep going. Keep up the normal, the real, 'cause all that other stuff just doesn't fit, it's not part of this life, even though it is all that you're left with in the end.

So I did. He was dead by four in the morning and I was at the bus stop by six. I sat quietly for the drive, watching the landscape roll by in darkness, watching the sky roll to bright, watching the day keep going on. I forgot my science project. And then we're there.

All the feet pounding and heads turning atop tense shoulders as we marched through the doors. We didn't look each other in eyes. Heads down, bowed, as we moved upstream against the current, as we just tried to avoid the predators. The shiny ones—new shoes, cunning smiles, twirl the hair, whisper, laugh, knock me down—those ones. Just keep going on.

We are sorted alphabetically into our seats. Roll call. Bell rings, eyes forward, everybody focus. Now isn't the time for hunger, or mourning, or cold. Now is the time that we are the same; the same kind of thoughts, the same kind of questions, but not out of turn. Keep your head down just so—not too far, they'll think you're sleeping, just far enough, so you don't stand out—and just get by. Now is the time for that.

It's preparation, daily practice, the liturgy of a bureaucratic society. Learn well here. You'll need it later on, when life after life fades away or is snuffed out and you don't know how to keep going, and then you remember to lower your eyes. Just keep going on. It's enough, maybe, perhaps, to just be good at surviving.

(I wonder what he would have thought of this age.)

TRIPTYCH
Or The Major Players of the Time that Shaped

he

I don't remember the precise sound of his voice, but I can show you
where his words landed when they bluntly impacted my childhood. This
mark, this fear, that obsession, this question, those ideas, what tools,
whose faith, which reasons, whose people?

I remember sitting beside him as we cruised down long roads
connecting nowhere to somewhere. No seat belts or air bags, no drive-
thrus, no places to be; only wide skies and thick air and ideas on all that
lies between the first breath and the last query.

One year before we left Louisiana, it snowed. We gathered the thin
spread of white from any surface and carefully piled it together until we
had enough stuff to form a tiny man with our gloved hands. He rested in
our freezer until spring when he was declared unseasonable and allowed
to melt in the sink.

her

After he ended, I once yelled at her for an hour, hoping to push
her to recognize that I was right there in front of her, attempting to
gain attention over the noise from her programs on the Christian
Broadcasting Network. I wanted to tell her about my science project but
she was riveted to the screen as Pat Robertson told stories all about how
the glory of God was found in another country, where the people there
were so simple they had no problems comprehending faith. As I strove to
earn observation, if not recognition, I remembered her acuity as it was
before him with a feeling too fraught to term *nostalgia*. Perhaps *anguish*?

Later that night, I thought about how long it would take for her to miss me if I left. But I knew I wouldn't go—who would finish cooking the meal?

I learned how to cook after my social worker brought over fresh herbs and ground spices for me to smell and taste and experiment with. As we chopped the herbs and their scent hit the air with an overwhelmingly earthy aroma, I met God. I found their glory in the steam that rose later from the pot as this stranger taught me about my people through chopping and dicing and stirring and savoring.

My mother said that it was good, but over-spiced.

they

More windows, more roads rolling by, more towns and stops, still between nothing and something, still trying to work through my questions, still trying to make something of myself, still trying to be in on the joke, still trying. Scents of motor oil and bodily excretions and moldy socks, of my favorite sweater and your leather jacket, of truck stop tea and fast food. This era had few flavors.

So many names, ways, places, the sameness of it all fell together until I could not tell one day apart from others of its kind. I could not find the right song, the right sound, and if I remembered which tune the right speaker fritzed out and I had to imagine the stereo.

My iron willfulness melted and my thick skin was stretched and pulled tight and my keen mind was dulled until I could easily please, and then one morning I awoke and realized that I had spent my life trying to live better than my father, and yet no glory could be found within me. And so I ran away.

They didn't miss me.

REFRAIN

I am a preacher man's only child.
He wanted a son,
but had a daughter.
He made me stone
then hit me hard to find the water.

Should I repeat the same mistake,
and miss the promised land?

(I have kept our
traditions
of sacrificing meat for the bones.

I am my own altar.)

TREE OF MEMORY

I planted you
in the yard by
the back gate.
The shade from
your branches
killed the
grass beneath,
but the moss
there grows well.

You are coolness
in the
summer heat
and a
nesting place
in spring.
Your leaves
blanket the
ground in
autumn, crackling
under my feet
as I carefully
take my next step.

Your naked
winter limbs
sway in cold winds
and cast
dark contours
on the snow
as the
moonlight shines
bright and the

earth glows
in a frigid sheen.
I believe you would
find your
final resting place
sufficient, if a bit
sentimental
—though
not quite
suitably
monumental.

You, like I,
were pulled
between
too many worlds.
Perhaps you will
find greater
peace
here
than you
did in
your other life.

Perhaps your
story always
ended here,
as a tree of
memory,
in a place
in-between.

I will
tell you this:
I understand
you now

in a way I
never did
before. I
remember
your last
story.

I tell it to
myself now,
as I sit
here in
your shade.
It is here
that I
have penned
these pages.

No one else
may recognize
you like this,
but I would
know your
presence
anywhere.

YOUR END

I am here, within my skin.
My soul was cramped in its
previous space.

I had smushed and pushed and chopped
myself until I could inhabit a small, quiet
place, but it was time for more room,
and a better view.

I found that after I removed
the bindings you used to
contain me,
my true form was unexpected.
My skin was quite raw.

I wonder if all of the names you gave me to keep are true names or
merely poor descriptors of an oddity. I may never fit your classifications.

I did not intend to misbehave.

But the rules you prescribed
only led me to fear my own shadow.
They did not teach me.

I am still only a suggestion of my
birthright. But I have years yet
to know my roots and claim them,
to see my extravagances and tame them.

I will not forget your end.

WHY

I was eleven. School had been underway for a few weeks. I entered my father's room, answering his summons with some trepidation, not knowing if I was receiving a harsh reprimand or a long list of tasks. But neither came that day.

For this memory, I cannot tell you the hue or intensity of the light that came through the curtains in his room. I did not make any observations of the books stacked by his bed. I remember the expression on his face, and I knew with gut-deep certainty that he was near death. I had known he was dying before, of course. But this time, I could feel death's approach.

And then, darkness. And his words, spoken in a measured cadence as he combed his fingers through my hair.

He told me his why. He showed me where his anger was rooted, when it was planted. He told me his fears: That he would never become more than he was and never knew what to do with a daughter. And he told me about his shame, which rapidly proliferated once he realized he had not protected me from his oldest worries.

Then he spoke of the future. His words sketched for me a map that would later become the guide for my quest. He told me he believed, more than he believed anything, that I would defeat the demons I was bequeathed. That I would overcome where he fell short, that I would live long enough to become the potential he would die before realizing.

At the time, I did not understand all of the self-hate that led him to speak these words to me. All I knew at that moment was the darkness of his room and the tangles his fingers caught combing through my hair, and it was there that I entered a cocoon for the first time.

Whoever you are, wherever you are, if you read these words and find that they are calling you into your own darkness, don't fear. I have been reshaped repeatedly, and it is from this destructive rebirth that I share my stories.

The travails that lead you to the dark places may be loud, brash, and cloying in turn. But the transformation itself is often relatively quiet, with few signs of foretelling that you are about to become a new being.

It does ache a bit when your bones begin to shift.

I recommend you enter the darkness of your cocoon with calm acceptance. If you've come this far, there is rarely time to turn back. (Do tell someone where you've gone—you may need another to remind you of your way home once you emerge.)

And when you break through the binds that held you for the change and face into the sun, with trembling balance as you adjust to the shifts in your weight from your new growth, it is pretty standard for your tender new skin to burn quickly. Take the appropriate precautions. You may want to shade your eyes.

What happens in the change? By what mechanisms does it occur? Those are questions for which I have no answers. If I knew them, I would be able to form a soul, and for all I have seen and done, I have never accomplished such a thing as that.

When will it happen? In my experience, it is rather a long while after one has entirely given up on the process. Perhaps your change will be kinder.

Where, as you know, is anywhere the crucible might find you.

Who will you be after? That is a great question.

I cannot give you your *why*. I would recommend that if you have the option to go ahead and commit to the transformation before you make any vows on someone's deathbed, do. But should that be your only option, such reasoning will suffice for a beginning.

Your reasons will come later.

How to Bury a Body

1. Dig a deep hole in the ground.
2. Do not climb in.

(It isn't your place.)

MYTHS, LEGENDS, & OTHER **TRUE TALES**

LEARN

I could leave you as the trope I found you, for you are too dead to argue, but that would teach me nothing beyond what happened.

What I need to learn is *why*. Beyond the line of my jaw and the scraggliness of my brows, I resemble you in other ways.

SHE'LL BE

The race to extend freedom saps the life out of us all, and yet we keep the pace, never slack behind, never fall back. The monsters at our heels will buy you a drink before taking the first bite.

Who knows if understanding will ever come our way? We may stand at the corner of the gravel road where it crosses the dirt path and wonder if our search was meaningful or if our wandering was in vain. And we may not find the key we swear was sitting on the table by the door when we left, where it is unfailingly placed.

I may not find reason or rhyme for the time that came before. I am stuck between fiction and lore, with no references to build the appendix of my very real life.

If I'm not real, I'd like to be a cowperson in a land with no cows, where the sunset stretches on endlessly and I can always keep up as I ride off into its brightness… the light will never completely fade. I'll ride out west on the mythical train. In an instant, forever from now, I'll arrive at my new land that I won't own and I'll give the coat off my back just to roam, just to unfocus my eyes for a while. The sun hurts them so.

I may jump from the train, put on my hat, and hide my eyes from your stare. And you'll never know it was me. But I'd soon give in to your Gene Autry smile, and we'd be off on our adventure 'round the world in a day.

Who knew you'd come home while running away?

ANDROID IN A HUMAN SUIT?

I am afraid
of both arachnids
and confining spaces

So, spelunking is out for me (or
"potholing" if you're from the
UK, according to Wikipedia)

Although I think bats are
fascinating creatures and I
love the dark, and quietness

And I would enjoy
working in a place with
consistent temperatures

It would be much more
predictable, I think,
than the moods of humans

All would be different if I were
an android and could detect
minute changes in your pulse

But alas, I am also human (I think)
so if you could simply explain
how you feel in words both

Specific and true
that would be nice
I would like that

HAUNTED BY MY OWN GHOST

I saw my own ghost.

I did not recognize her at first
but it was her eyes,
her wrists,
her movement quality—
she was cagey
but also bold.

I tried to take a photo and
capture the moment.
Give proof for the ghost hunters.
But the film failed to develop.

What would you say
to your ghost
if they are here?
What do you believe you will miss
after your day comes?
What names will you forget?
What places have you inhabited
that will be as if they never were?

If you could bring your ghost home,
what would you serve for your meal?
What do you think you would care to watch yourself taste
when you are nothing but bones and dust and vapor?

I have poured tea,
in case my ghost returns to me.

You would never take me for the
villain. I have long perfected
my winning smile, cunningly
deployed when your wrath is
simmering.

I will never give myself away in
my long monologues. I design my
words to obscure my meaning
and soothe your senses.

But I have plans—meticulously
rendered with a robust strategy—
and I will press onward with an
unfailing strength of will.

You might halt a skirmish here or
there, and I've already decided
which valleys and hills to concede
graciously. But the war is mine.

The outcome was predicted long
ago, and who am I to turn away
from such flowery forewarning?
Who am I to thwart the plans for
supremacy?

I am merely a tool for history's
reproach. I began this campaign
on a whim, but I will see it
through to its end.

HOW TO PASS

As Told to Me by Many Voices

You must practice these disciplines daily.

First, you must forever remember your place. Know your better and your lesser kin. Know that all that your mind can conceive must be tightly bound in a polite and yielding skin, or you will give away the game.

Second, you must cut away the extra. All that does not fit the mold given to you by the victors. Trim your hips, your lips, your thighs. Dress modestly and hide your shape; never allow your body to seduce unless there is something to gain from your efforts.

Third, you must practice forgetting. No matter your fears or the shame that this chosen ignorance may cost you. Abandon your ancestors and make a new line.

You will learn to lie with a mild tone and a humble eye. If you cannot falsify the truth well, hold your tongue. Many things may be forgiven if you clothe yourself in meekness.

You must always behave. Above all, you must never allow your anger to surface. Once it breaks through the bindings, it will color your countenance and make your gaze too bold for one such as you.

After all, you're white enough, aren't you? To choose a new name?

BROTHER MINE

My brother
and I
adopted each other
one evening during
the time in
which we
resided near
the beach. We
found ourselves
on top of a tall,
wobbly bookcase,
in a mutually
unplanned attempt
to flee
the ominous approach
of a spider
on the floor.

We had escaped with
one giant leap.
We looked at each other
and then back
at the spider,
and knew in that moment
that we were siblings
separated by
parentage,
time,
and
place.

Several years later,
we still avoid killing each
other,
and also spiders.

We took
within us the
distinct heritages
we inherited
and planted
upon our skins
the words with
which we each
were named
until we were
well laden with
overgrown weeds.

And then, we cut
each other free
until we could stand,
ripped and bloody,
dragging ruined flesh,
but unburdened
and nameless.

(Sarcasm is to
cut with sharp
words.)

As time provided
balm I
learned to laugh
at your jokes,
and you

learned
that I do not
lie, though my
specificity
may slice deep.

We have pulled
together
a family of
torn and broken
roots
and somehow two
strays hold the
center,
while others provide
the strength.

If it is true that blood
is thicker than
milk,
our wounding aims
struck true.

NEMESIS

Sometimes you are
sharp and unyielding—
you poke through my resolve
and find my weak places.

Sometimes you are dull
and pervasive,
swelling from my gut
and spreading through my bones.

Sometimes you are pulsing
and loud
and bright
and crushing
and I am left with few reserves.

I am told to meditate on life's
deeper meanings,
to remember a time without you
and focus on how I felt then
and let that feeling overpower
you. But I do
not remember anything
of the time before you.

They say I must not surrender to you, that I should
foil your efforts with balms and scents
with teas and poses
with pills and patches
but I have found nothing to dissuade
your onslaught.

I am told that my faith will heal me but I have held
on for days on end despite you, yet still you are present.

Each day, you arrive promptly.

You press in on all sides
regardless of my actions.

You sing haunting melodies in my dreams,
and you have pushed me to the verge, to the
place where I can see through the
thin veil that divides this time
from the next one.

I cannot defeat you or push you back,
so I will sink into you.

I will wrap myself around you
and squeeze at your depths
and change your nature.

You must remember that I have spent my life fighting you,
so I have been trained well to match you.

You have never broken my will and I
do not believe that now will be
an exception,
as my will is a gift
and you cannot receive.

You strive to change me,
to make me
small
confined
diminished.

But instead, I will transform you.

You will be broadened
deepened

expanded
explored.

I will know my enemy.

You must know by now that our struggle
has made me into one who will hold fast.

Let us see which one of us lasts and finds meaning.

You may take your time.

I will wait.

My meaning is found in the stillness
and silence of the times in between.
Your meaning is only found within me.

Who would you say is the victor here?

WITCH'S TALE

A voice called to me, called me by name, as I lay prostrate on the floorboard of the very back seat of our old station wagon. It was summer in rural Louisiana. We traveled to a camp meeting. My dog cuddled close as we both panted, the empty two-liter of soda a distant memory of a time when we were not thirsty.

Sweat soaked my skin, light burned my eyes, I felt faint. My vision blurred, my tongue stuck to the roof of my mouth, and there my parietal eye opened, and I saw all of time.

As the woman with an issue of blood was healed when she touched the hem of Christ's robes, my mother's barrenness became fruitfulness when I was conceived in the autumn of 1979. My mother had always wanted a little girl.

I was born in July with a broken heart. The valves did not do what valves should do, and my blood pumped the wrong way. They flew me to New Orleans for urgent care, but by the time I arrived, the hole in my heart had closed.

No one was surprised when this miracle child, the one who never should have breathed, was given a divine spark from birth. No one was surprised when the hole in my heart closed by no other power than the hand of God.

As I was baptized and water pooled from my skin, I heard a voice call me by name. This voice told the story of who I was, how I came to be, what would happen, and how I would last to the end. I knew then that my magic was strong.

The ghosts of times long past have sustained me.

The first genuine test of my gifts came when I willed that my father should no longer waste away from pain. I wrote a story of death with a fair ending, proper origins and context, and spoke it to the air.

I don't remember a time in which I did not know that I should have never been.

After he perished and we buried his cold and waxy form, I stood there in my navy dress and black patent shoes—the people around me fading from view—I knew that I had seen true what I had chosen. I smiled, even as I watched him descend into the ground and give me his ghost.

I have wrought destruction through storms and floods.

I have brought droughts and danced to bring the rains again. I create and destroy, heal and impair, bind and release with impunity.

Such early experience with death drove me to chase a well-structured mortality. I trained endlessly, running mile after mile, beating my flesh, tearing holes in my socks and in my skin, in hopes that my penance would delay my failing as long as possible. I built as much strength into my muscles as I could before the illness stole my deep breaths. My plans were foiled as I broke my bones and nearly lost my sight.

As I stood again next to death, this time my own, nearly chosen and yet hindered, the voice spoke again. The voice told me to prophesy, bring life to dead bones, tell stories the specters had forgotten, and remind you of who you are.

And so, I ripped my soul from my flesh so that I could wander the earth in the night without waking you. I learned new spells from the stars and the monsters of the deep. I have forgotten entire centuries, but still weaved my path through history enough times that the patterns became clear, and I could create them with my hands and my words and my tones.

In the beginning, the very first time the calling came to me to tell me how I would suffer but endure, I knew. Before I was old enough to understand that I was a seer, one given the powers to discern the slightest thread of light in the darkest of dark, I knew. I knew I would find you and bind myself to you, and together, we would remake the skies.

Lay your head down; I will run my fingers through your hair and whisper a tale of when the twilight will stretch and pull at a tight angle until a dim light blankets the Earth and the tides cease. I will spread balm on your scars, breathe cool air into your lungs, and choreograph a fantastical dream so you may never wonder where I went, despite what the years might bring.

My heart is weak. I still run as often as I am able, despite the infirmity that has pervaded me, despite the pain that runs with me. You are the pain I choose.

Pack your bags; we're heading out this weekend. I'll bring snacks and water, and when you stare out through the windshield as you steer us down wide highways leading from nowhere to wherever and I see your focus falter, I will reveal the timely sustenance packed away in my purse. Don't forget to quench your thirst after a while. It will be a long drive.

RETURN TO THE WATER

Your cathedrals cannot hold me, your churches do not often welcome me, but it is no matter.

I returned to the water.

The winds sing my hymns, and I am new each day as I sweat under the sun; I soak in the mists of the cosmos each night as I sleep nestled in the stars.

The trees give sermons from their long memories in the creaking of their branches, sharing their stories through their roots and the chemicals released into the air from the pores of their skin. The fungi record their canon, as many ancient giants no longer cast tall shadows but do nourish the grove in their decay.

The birds flit from branch to branch and share gossip, calling out songs of food, shelter, succor, and warnings of predators. The butterflies land on my skin in the sunlight. The moths are drawn to the light of the fires in the night.

When I need to be baptized again, I return to the water and sing the song that reminds me that this precious liquid binds us to the earth that grew us. My veins are patterned after the river systems connecting far-flung soils to the oceans surrounding us all.

Nature does not mind my broken body or weak heart. The Earth does not hold it against me that I now amble through its fields, though I used to run those same paths with a rapid and steady rhythm. I am bent like the fallen branches; I am smoothed like river rocks; I am akin to the wrinkled tree trunks telling of their ages seen with their rings, I am cousin to the elm that comforted me during many dark years.

When my days conclude, I will return to the sanctuary of the ground. As my flesh decays, my soul will descend to the depths along the roots of the trees until I reach hidden streams where I will swim freely without tiring. My ghost may never leave the forest. My epitaph shall be this:

"She lived a good, good life."

ECCLESIASTES

We are all extinguished at varying rates.

The aches and pains of life will compound until our flesh gives way to dust.

What is the meaning? There is none.
Burn your years away and watch the flames.

Tell your stories.
Bring s'mores.

Back in the day,
I cared what others thought of me.

THINK ABOUT WHAT JUST HAPPENED

TRUE FORM

You might have
caught
             on

                      by now
but
my true
form is that of

a nine-f oot tall,

purple,
fire-breathing drago n.

I chose a small er form
for ev eryday wear, as my
wingspan make s it difficult to pass
through doors. And
be sides, typing wit h
             tal ons
             is next to
i mpossible for m   e.

But on dark, stormy nights
or those with the full
light of the
             moo n, if

you
are outside, you might

feel an ominous shadow passing
overhead.

Don't worr y, it's just me.
            Hanging o ut.

I probably won't
hurt you. The

evide nce for
those fi ery deaths for

which I
was blame d was purely
            circ umstantial.

PLEASE UNDERSTAND

Neatly trim your
humanness, shed
your glory—no one
wants to
see all that.

Edit your story.

Remove all the smells
and sounds.

Quietly behave
as if you are immortal
(but also willing to go
gently, when it's
your time).

Leave no footprints
or tire treads.

Stay in your lane—remain
within the category in which
we placed you at birth.

You may undergo one
transformation, from
an approved list of changes:
fat to skinny, old to young,
poor to rich, ill to healed,
plain to beautiful,
et cetera.

More than one
would be gauche.

This is why we cannot

break the patterns
set for us by
the founding fathers:
we cannot be bothered.

It would be too far
past modern,
it would be too strange.

And when we move
into our spaceships
we will want some
familiar trappings.

Change
makes us itchy.

You do understand,
of course?

*(If you seek further
meaning on these harsh
truths, consider the
source.)*

NAKED

I sometimes use my words
to obscure my true
form.

This method is effective
because I tell you the
truth.

I have no qualms
with giving you
an obscenely
naked view,
but this is only
to distract you
from looking into
my eyes.

This strategy
of simulated vulnerability
only holds up when I can
avoid direct
questioning.

Illusions fall
apart
when the
house lights
are turned on.

I am a mutt,
a mongrel,
so mixed I am nothing
but not allowed to
be everything.
In no particular order
I am English
and West African and
Chitimacha and
French and Nachitoches
and Islenós and Norwegian
and Mission Indian
and possibly Choctaw but
we aren't sure. Oh, and Dutch.

I think that's it? Oh! There's my Chinese great-great grandfather from Cuba. His relationship to me is a more recent discovery. His story may be more interesting than mine, but I haven't learned it yet, so until that time, enjoy the one you're stuck with.

I remember the day that I took my first standardized test and realized that the system wanted me to erase someone, anyone, everyone but one so that I would fit more neatly into the sorting bins, so my story could be told with one well-shaded bubble. No one wants to think about how you don't get as mixed as I in one generation or two, or three. People have been coming together outside color lines in this country for a long time.

I carry stories in my psyche and my gut and my bones. I sweat out my fears and desires to be something with a name, to remember a time when I heard the words, "Oh, don't you look just like your parents." People can see it now, when I bring out the pictures, now that the baby fat is truly gone and you can see my father's bone structure and my mother's nose and my auntie's smile. But my father and aunties are all dead, so it means less now to me than it would have then.

What percentages am I? Well, I am a third Cyclops on my mother's side, a fifth Vulcan on my father's, and part Coyote and also unicorn and all human and all dragon and I dare you to tell me any different. I do not care for your fractions. I am my stories; they are the sinew that holds me together. As I have written elsewhere, I am born of slave and master, captive and captor, highborn but forever displaced. What that means is that I refuse to erase any of my ancestors no matter how much I love or despise them or feel generally apathetic toward them or wish they kept better records or wish they could have stayed with their families even if that would have erased me.

I have been told that in the future, we will all be mixed. But those who tell me this long for a day in which we can wipe away our racial past and all have good hair. I am here to tell you that is never going to happen, because we have been mixed for centuries, and I will not allow you to forget that. I am sorry our people did not give you a more straightforward story to digest. You will endure. I promise.

So when people, strangers, acquaintances, ask me what I am, I will look them dead in the eyes and tell them I am a story that many would like to ignore, but one which will lodge in their brains until they ask better questions.

Or, I could say that I am chilled black tea with sweetness added in the boil and spices and fruit juice that some people call tea and hot tea with a bit of milk and green tea brewed strong and bitter to better savor the aroma and tea that has been sorted and dried and packaged and sent far away from the places I grew. Sip that truth for a while, and see how it sets you.

NO CONTEXT

Or Some Things Have Humor and Many Also Hurt
(with few if any actual transitions)

I once jumped off a 40-foot cliff into cold water after a two-hour hike, though I am not a good swimmer, and have Raynaud's phenomenon (a condition which causes a hypothermic response in mild temperatures), just to get out of what I perceived to be a futile and never-ending conversation about who was going to jump off the cliff first. I did not want to go cliff jumping or hiking to begin with. The water was, as I had feared, quite cold.

When I was a child, I was incredibly literal. Thus, when I was finally made to understand a joke about the archaic spelling of ketchup, or "cats-up," I found the resulting pun about a feline in a tree so humorous that I giggled to myself every time I ate French fries until I was about twenty.

I have a relatively poor record of accurately interpreting the futures I see. I also have terrible luck. I do not bet unless it is worth going all in. I also never bet on horses. However, perhaps I am nearing the time when my fortunes shift, in which case I'm putting everything on a horse named By Any Means 'cause, hell, you only live once.

The most unusual scar I have is from a bus backfiring on my left thigh, leaving me with second– and third-degree burns and a smattering of carbon particles just under the skin. This happened on a youth trip on the Texas side of the border, and this is apparently when many people learned that I am rather funny when under the influence.

I am currently under the influence. God, I hope this is working.

I dreamt that Nashville flooded two years before it happened. I am still more than a little mad at God about that.

When I was given glasses in the third grade, I was immediately teased for being "four-eyed." The teasing did not offend me because I was being insulted. It offended me because I had learned in my optometrist's office that the major parts of the eye are the pupil, cornea, lens, retina, choroid, optic nerve, and vitreous humor, and thus, the bullies' taunts were far too limited in scope to be remotely accurate. I don't have four eyes. I have four *lenses*.

I developed claustrophobia the time my cousins shoved me into the pantry at my paternal grandfather's house. They told me they would "wipe that smug look off my face." They used a broom handle to teach me that some men will not respect the sanctity of my body. My grandfather was heating stew on the stove nearby and laughed when I cried. I remember later sitting at the dinner table and rubbing my right thumb over a knot in the table's wood in a figure-eight pattern to keep from flying apart.

Though many have tried,
no one has ever wiped that smug look off my face.

I hate sweeping.

My maternal grandmother once told me, "I do hope you grow into your physical oddities, for I am certain that no man will appreciate the sharpness of your tongue. And you're going to have to marry rich because artists are, appropriately, compensated poorly. Or, you could go to law school." I managed to find a man who likes the way I look (and likes my tongue) so I think that one worked out in my favor. And it was purely by accident.

We are not wealthy. I know a few lawyers.

I am not afraid of most predatory animals. I do have a somewhat
incapacitating fear of any insect with more than six legs. I find them
to be overly ostentatious. And I can walk sideways just fine on two legs,
even with a cane, so I don't see the fuss about having eight or more. I'm
sure you saw this coming, but this is why I can never go to Australia.

There was a kid in my middle school who made a crude joke about
my appearance on the day my father died. You're right, that is kind
of horrible, but the story doesn't end there. I did not forgive him and
proceeded to show him the acidity of my discourse with cruel words for
years. I learned of my error in my thirties while watching an episode
of 30 Rock in which Liz Lemon realizes that you can be the one who is
bullied and also the bully at the same time. In summary, he said one
mean thing to me. I said countless mean things to him.

I was always afraid of dying. I was sure it would hurt more than
anything, and I would hate for that to be my last memory.

When I was eighteen, I woke up in the hospital with no memory as to
why I was there, as an ER surgeon stitched my left eyelid back together.
He handed me a mirror and told me to observe the neatness of his
stitches, and it was then that I noticed the giant dent in my forehead.

I realized later that I could have died on the side of the road, just before
the toll booth on the way to Tulsa from Oklahoma City, and thus, dying
was probably going to be a lot like life. That is to say, generally in direct
contrast to my original plans.

I may be ushered from this realm into the next by people who
possess no immediate need to respect my personal space or to offer
pertinent information in a timely manner. Of this possibility, I am well
acquainted.

But I still don't want to leave you.

I have been accused of stealing, being a witch, performing animal sacrifices, running an orgy cult, physically embodying the spirit of Jezebel, using mind control, and methodically removing a former friend from all of my pictures, among other things.

As a small child, I did steal bubble gum from grocery stores on more than one occasion. According to my parents, the only things more inappropriate than a lady chewing bubble gum are ladies wearing jeans or not knowing when to keep their legs closed. I wasn't daring enough at the time for the jeans, or the sex, as I was four, and lived in a reasonably warm climate, so I went with the easiest path to rebellion against gender norms as they were presented to me at the time. We couldn't afford the bubble gum anyway, so I didn't ask.

In eighth grade, I learned that I lived in one of the safest places in the world. Our distance from the coasts and the surrounding terrain made it so difficult it was basically impossible for a foreign invader to attack our home.

A year later, I learned that I did not, in fact, live in the safest place in the world when a white supremacist bombed my city.

I sometimes fantasize about being an atheist—or even just an affable, mild-tempered agnostic.

I once had a friend who explained the difference between being factually correct and morally right; let me tell you, we are all delighted that this conversation happened.

However, no one told me that I could be a bit of an asshole until I was almost thirty. They hinted towards the issue, as if I have ever been a person who appreciates encountering hints outside of a crossword puzzle. Just think for a minute about all the time I could have put towards not being an asshole had I been plainly informed of this truth far sooner and if I hadn't spent all that time being paranoid about accidentally starting an orgy cult.

If you ask for my input, I will try to be as specific as possible to avoid confusion and limit unexpected outcomes.

I cannot handle the sound of teeth scraping on a fork. But like, *really*.

When I speak of my father, I am sometimes asked what I think about him and his legacy. To answer this question, I must illustrate the vast distance between his wisdom and depravity.

Once, he told me that regardless of my heritage, I should not say the n-word as no one needed to hear that word coming out of a face that looked like mine. This is easily actionable and both compassionate and prudent advice.

Another time, he woke me at four-thirty in the morning on a school day to tell me that his cancer had come out of remission because my mother was speaking in tongues[1], and God was punishing him as the head of our household. He then informed me that if I told anyone about what he said to me that morning, he'd kill my dog.

In summary, my experiences with him were a bit of a mixed bag.

I am often accused of having rather extreme motivations for fairly innocuous actions. I seldom defend myself.

I once watched an entire procession of clowns pass behind my friend as she told me about what I think was a very traumatic experience involving farm animals—a whole bunch of clowns—she never noticed.

---

[1]   Phrase of speech; (to) speak in an unknown language during religious worship, regarded as one of the gifts of the Holy Spirit (Acts 2). *From Oxford Languages.*

No one mentioned anything, so I wasn't entirely sure if I was still in this reality or not.

So yes, I absolutely did not take your feelings into account when I said that thing I don't remember saying while I wasn't listening, and that was wrong.

I didn't realize that my grandmother made me hate my body by hating all of my physical attributes which she worried would give away the secret that underneath the pale skin, I was also a person of color. I have decided that she was full of shit.

This is mildly ironic as when she died she had advanced colon cancer, among other things, so I have decided to honor the most valuable contribution she made to my life, which was to do her best to ensure I did not go hungry often.

I have a back-up plan for everything, including the end of our present society and the ensuing chaos that will result. Now, before that brings you any comfort, let me tell you that my second-level backup plan for the end of current things is to find a cave in which to compile near-endless volumes of nihilistic, free-verse poetry, until I die of complications from trying to maintain an allergy-safe diet without Google. At least one volume will remain forever unfinished.

My child once told me that her favorite thing about me is that I never give anyone false hope.

I regularly practice telekinesis in case it starts working. (It's still not working.)

Despite my years of Sunday School, I am not a very good Evangelical because the foundations of my faith are not in the years I have spent dissecting theology but rather in a few mystical experiences which utterly redefined me. I have no idea how to convince other people to have mystical experiences with God and have thus deemed the entire pursuit of Evangelicalism to be more than a little futile. Yes, this is rather vain of me.

When I die, I have instructed those who remain to bury me in a haunted forest. I have already begun stories about how my ghost haunts forests for those who survive me to pass on to the next generations. I plan to end the collection of said stories on a cliff-hanger and dedicate the series to my fourth-favorite grandchild to make them all wonder. Should my child choose not to procreate, as is her right, I will hold an open casting call for at least five grandchildren, so the whole conceit[2] truly works.

Should I die before my due time, perhaps even before you read this, my ghost is right outside your window, looking in. Should you have no windows, never fear; I can walk through the walls.

I've always been a long-term planner.

I remember watching episodes of Star Trek: The Next Generation and observing how Captain Picard listened to his crew. Like, really listened, with eye contact and everything, no matter their gender or species. I always wanted to meet a man like that.

I ended up marrying a man who is a great listener, a stellar listener, really the best listener, but who almost never remembers what I have said shortly thereafter. I should have been more specific.

I never had a goldfish before.

---

[2]   Yes, this is an archaic usage of the word conceit, meaning "a [overly] fanciful metaphor." I generally prefer a play on words over conforming to modern English. But sometimes I'm also archaic.

MINE, THROUGH THE AGES

flint

I would sink within your skin
evaporate from deep within you,
spread my soul on the
surface of your lungs,
only to end as you exhaled
and rise again as one who has
lived and seen the beauty
of our frail mortality.

Sometimes, in the afterwards,
I lie there as you doze and
read the lines on your face
as they tell me the story
of your life.

I never want to forget the
furrows and phrases that make
you who you are.

copper

You taught me how to say "I am beautiful"
and this will remain no matter how either of us end.

iron

I thought I would be perfect before I found you.

In my head, all would be laid out in front of me and I would never look
back. I would be calm and collected, and the temper that had burned
within me would be stilled. There would be no harsh words flung from
its flames.

Then fire met fire, and iron met iron. You were cold when you were alone just as I was. The facade rarely gave way and we both thought we were opaque.

I remember the night you first saw me. It was dark in the room and the moonlight shone in and I hid my face from you while I cried—I hated to cry.

There have been years of words and nights with tears. I never wanted to grieve but you fought me for it, and I met you with everything you threw. You dared me to retaliate and I remembered that life had not killed me yet and I always come back from a fall. I showed you that fighting was so close to dancing and you learned to hold me close when I lost control. That's how it was.

I'll never beat you, and we'll never give in. As we mend the wounds others leave, the day comes and we remember why we were made to fight; why we never surrender. I'll stand with my back to yours and I'll not fear what's behind me again.

The fires are dwindling. We have replaced our facades with our own faces. We will keep trading strength for strength. My temper has been tamed and I am not so afraid to weep though I will likely continue to apologize for doing so. You'll still hold me at night and we'll whisper our dreams as we watch each other sleep (when you don't snore).

Slowly we trade the fight for the dance. My youthful ideals are beginning to seem shallow as lines form and gray takes hold in your beard. I am young and old. You are old and young.

I will still laugh when no one knows why and you will still tell me horrible jokes.

The sharp iron will lie cool by the fire.

I have a picture of you and I sitting on a patio on a cool, rainy day. Shortly after, I talked you into taking a walk and letting the drops fall as they may and drip smoothly down our forms. You thought it was a bit ridiculous but humored me, as always. Our shoes squished as we splashed and my hair frizzed as the light faded and the day fell to twilight. You caressed my hand, allowing my thumb to tuck into your palm in that way you find so strange. It seemed too good to be, but it was no distant dream. I was right there.

I MARK TIME WITH OBSERVATIONAL STATEMENTS

My first fear was of eternity.

You know the wait for Christmas morning, or how long it takes to make caramel popcorn? Or have you felt the span of time and space between the first word spoken in blessing over a meal and the last, the aroma of the food so strong you can almost taste it?

Waiting is an ache that may never be relieved, or a heartsickness that will grip you in your depths until the moment passes and the wrapping is torn and the caramel drips from your fingers and you savor the first bite of the flavors you have anticipated.

And then satisfaction, completion, fullness. Or, ill-fitting socks in your stocking, burned fingers, overcooked vegetables—but at least the wait is over. You can move past it, turn on the TV, and lose yourself in harsh colors and high-pitched voices that tell stories in declarative statements depicting the defeat of evil and restoration of normality until next time.

Or perhaps you wait for something that will never come. That is a different ache entirely.

Sometimes, when I can't sleep—which is always—I stare into the darkness above my bed. If you stare long enough, the ceiling disappears. I can see the clouds, the stars, the center of it all. I breathe as quietly as I can, as shallowly as possible, so as to not disturb the landscape. I wait.

When my father spoke of eternity and an endless stretch of time with God, all I could think was that Christmas would never come, nothing would be sweet again, and I would never be full. I wondered what we would talk about for eternity if there were nothing to watch. Are there empty moments to be filled in forever? Will I need to sleep?

My second fear was of dying.

Not death or being dead, but rather that infinitesimal moment when your connection to this world is snapped, and you cross over to the next. (Whatever that might be, if there are streets of gold or enlightenment or a new age or nothing, it will be foreign. You won't know the customs. I assume one may adjust.) I fear the transition.

And your last memory of the world that was, the last bit of it you hold in your hands and breathe in your lungs and pump through your veins in the present, is an ache that will never be relieved.

When I was little, maybe five or six, I dreamt I was shot in the heart. I was standing on the side of the road somewhere in Texas; I felt the tearing of my flesh and saw my blood seep into the ground. My knees buckled and I fell onto my face. My vision blacked out. I woke up, and it was Sunday.

My third fear was of spiders. You never know where you'll find them.

CLOSETS

My house was clean when
you came over,
but I did not show
you the closets.

There, I have
kept refuse from
a thousand years
of
birth and loss.

I did not want
you to
think less of me,
so I kept those
doors closed and the
spaces dark.

HOW TO HOST A SOIRÉE

One must savor the flavors of the
various dishes that life
presents—savory to
sweet to bitter. Add a little salt
and spice and pour the wine.

You will find one can swallow
most anything—it is all in the
balance of tastes on the tongue.

Never underestimate the
effect of skillful seasoning as you
prepare your moldering
trimmings.

If you piece the meal together
for presentation over sustenance,
your fellow guests will effusively
praise their every bite.

The amusement of dissecting the
flavors—naming them
to showcase your elocution—is
well known.

Do not neglect
a pinch of poison in each serving.

When the concluding course comes,
you will be accustomed to the taste.
As that final ration of toxin spreads
through your veins you can relish
your last bite and comfort yourself
in the knowing
that at least you ate well.

GOOD PEOPLE

Or, When You Pray for Me, Remember This

I have known some good people who kept me fed and
clothed and warm, sometimes, but who always
made sure I remembered that I did not
earn it—could not deserve it—for
my life is meaningful
but rather expensive.

I have known some good people ready to pray
for me, anytime, but who grip their beliefs
tightly with their eyes firmly shut
when my mere presence
reminds them we are each
of us mortal.

I have known some good people who read
my words and think,
Oh, you poor dear,
how you suffer so,
but do not care to see the nuances
my stories display.

I have more to say.

I have known some good people who find me inspiring, but that
inspiration must not be anything close to divine;
it does not seem to motivate alterations
to their words or to
their actions.

So when you say, "I pray for you often"
or, "but I'm a good person"
I am rarely (but sometimes) moved.

HOW TO TELL IF YOU'RE STILL ALIVE

Because Sometimes People Will Ask You to Be Sure

(Inspired by that one extremely helpful emergency room doc of mine who wasn't sure.)

Are you still capable of laughter?

I mean, even if the world is crumbling,
as society gives way?

Are you still able to seep with tears?

I mean, even if you feel that
you should be dehydrated to the point of death?

Do you still feel your anger?

I mean, even if you have already raged
and the world has yet to change?

When you can't do any of these things,
are you able to forgive yourself?

Or at least consider that it might be nice
if your mind didn't rule your
body so fearfully?

You're probably alive,
but don't take my word for it.

I would test this by trying out
some actions.

For example,
can you breathe?

Even if you need help to do so?

Then yes, you are alive.

The gap that follows
represents
the many loops
spent
in silence.

LAST TASKS BEFORE LEAVING **TOMORROW**

TO BE FREE

Or, An Outline of Ruminations on "Winged Creatures"

I had read about birds, looked at illustrations of birds, and occasionally watched public access shows about birds (told to me in voices with crisp accents and firm tones).

The day I was given glasses and learned to see clearly occurred in the eighth year of my life.

On that day, I witnessed a bird in flight.

To see another creature so keenly—I perceived the texture of its feathers, the light in its eyes, the sharpness of its beak. I observed the stillness of the air that the bird seemed to take within itself as it perched on the branch. And then, suddenly, it reached with broad wings into the sky and fled the weight of the earth.

I loved the moment between stillness and flight—the slight twitch that displayed the decision to fly.

Flight. The noun took action before my eyes.

We have quantified and categorized seemingly infinite varieties of these winged creatures. Peering into their feathers and bones, we have traced their lineage to the thunder-footed beasts that roamed the earth in long-ago times.

Who named the birds?

Did anyone ask them what they call themselves?

What do they think of us?

We, who lusted after flight for millennia until we built ourselves a plane?

And now, to fly means waiting in lines and removing our shoes.

I wonder how many birds are born with a fear of heights. Indeed, a few young hatchlings have resisted their parents' incentives to leave their comfortable nests for food.

Would the terror ever fade?

Or could one simply choose to fly without ever looking at the ground?

What motivated the emu to evolve away from its flight to become the second-fastest runner among flightless birds?

Was it fear or comfort?

Though they tower over their flying cousins when standing,

they will never again see the world from above.

I wonder what they see when they look at the sky.

TRUE STORY

We have never escaped the Dark Ages. We still tell our children frightening stories so that we might teach them from an early age whom and what they should fear and hate and how much love and hope they are allowed to take.

We still arm them, not with swords but with words disgorged into the air—words designed to suck out the power from the opposing side, words crafted to leave marks—and well-stocked armaments so our actions back up our threats (but rarely our promises).

We still believe in monsters and hauntings and dreadful creeping things, things that might slip in while we sleep and ruin us, steal our potential, change us into something too foreign and unlike our kind, something that will never be allowed to go home again.

We still forcefully take what is ours. We still hide away our precious things in hopes that we can pass on the fruits of our greed to the next generation.

We still look at the stars and fear what they might foretell, fear the curses that will befall us if we know the true nature of the world.

We have lit every corner and crevice we could wire, yet we are still afraid of the dark.

Do you not understand the story of the Tower of Babel, the mighty rise of a structure designed to conquer the fear of the unknowable? And then we were scattered, for it is better to wander in truth than to decide that you have built the highest tower that could ever be built.

You wish for a hope that will guide you, light you, comfort you; you want answers that will order the fates in definitive lines, for a mage to weave spells to heal your blindness, for prophets to tell you you'll have more than you need when you get to where you are going.

I will be of no such comfort. I will tell you that you will be destroyed in the night, you will lose everything you have worked so hard to store away, all of what you produce will decay, and eventually, you will be forgotten.

You will never have enough. You will never arrive. Everything you have built rests on tremulous foundations.

Build your towers of rhetoric and righteousness and live securely in your high places. And when the confusion comes, when all you think you know fails you, when you are sent to the next place and don't understand anything of what just happened, don't say I didn't warn you.

Is there a better way, you might ask? Of course. But that truth is not mine to give you. My journey was born from a leap of faith, fueled by the wild Spirit, and I cannot presume to define your steps, elaborate on your motivation, or give you the source of your beliefs.

I will tell you that I have fallen from great heights and did not learn that I could fly. I have no wings.

I will tell you that it was at that moment when I crashed into the earth that I decided to believe.

I will tell you my faith is marred by deep indentations from my fingernails.

I will tell you that this morning, I laughed.
That is all I will say about that.

EMUNAH

When I wanted
to learn to be
faithful,
I carefully placed
my feet in the
indentations left
by your steps,
as you trod the
same path for
days without end.

Taking this
lesson with
me,
I held fast
when the winds
came and the
storms
descended.

When your arms
grow weary
and your heart
forgets
the magic
you wield,
I will bring
you to a resting
place
and lift your
arms high,
and we will
see what
may happen then.

TRUE POWERS

(this is what happened after)
If you should forget your power,
it will escape you and cause untold destruction.
What should create will hurt.

When it happens, as it will, despite you, stop there and observe.
Note who you are, where you are. Perceive the dirt that is at the base of
everything we have built and of which we are so proud.

Remove your shoes, for the times in which we separate light from dark
are sacred times. It may rain.

Place your bare feet on the wet earth and try to feel
as tall as you felt before.
You'll find yourself sinking into the ground.
Like a person. Not so big, not so small.

Your power will grow.
Not to make you stand tall.
nor to debase yourself as lower than low.

But right there—toes in the dirt,
face to the sky, wind in your hair,
bugs on your skin, grass tickling
your shins, rain on your face,
your power grows—and you
can grasp it, hold it,
change it, create with it.

(this is what came before)
I didn't know
that you loved me.

It wasn't until my beliefs failed me
that I realized I had forgotten my power,
and so I used my words as blunt tools
against you.
If the years have
blessed me, it is only with
hindsight.

And so I walked in the dirt. I stood in the field next
to the old oak tree and
felt the wind rip anguish from me.
I could not resist.

There I was joined by the hands the wind brought me.

Hands in my hands,
hands pressing gently
on my back,
hands wiping my face,
hands leading me onward.

(now)
Hands are dirty.
Remember your places.
Your power grows from there.

SHOULD'VE | BRAINFOG | GENTRIFIED

1

To conceive clearly is not
to know—it is
to pull and push
and poke and shove
the ideas we have
collected as adults
and consider them again
with the mind of a child
and remember that we are
so small, so tiny, such
a bare speck on the ground,
such a short tree, such a
violent ape.

Wonder again, question
and fear and wrestle and
demand and cower and deflect.

Safe does only what safe
knows best.

But what
does safe become?

2

I am a summary of my
family's history
Cliff notes for the years of
cognitive dissonance,
innocent hopes,
cynical dreams.

Losses beyond my own imagining
Born pressed into a small
form with thick skin
and a bleeding heart.
(I mean a heart
that was literally leaking.)
I am tinted with cerulean hues
pooling and cooling in my slow,
bumbling feet, held firmly
within my practical shoes.

Time slowed down for me,
as I evolved backwards:
from dancing
to running
to stumbling
to crawling on all fours,
until at last I found
the ground
and begged it to hold
the weight of me.

I feared I might fall through
the thin crust that divides
above from below.

What once was so near to me is
now placed too far away
and I can't walk that far,
unassisted.

Nor can I reach up so very high.

But I am not broken down, yet,
though I am broken in—
my tissues inflamed with the
heat of resistance
against the forces that strive
to reduce me.

For all it does to remember...
sometimes, I remember.

Sometimes,
it is lost from my mind so
thoroughly I am certain it
will never be discovered
until long after I've moved
round the bend
and this old place is torn down
for a new tall and skinny.

What have I lost?

I can't recall it.

But I suspect it dealt
with definitions
and certainties
and this morning.

It will come back to me,
I am sure.

Like all things
have a way of
coming back
to be found,
crumbling and
stained and sticky
at the bottom of
my old evening clutch.

3
I wanted to shelter you from
the real composition of the world

and so I clothed you in magic
and dreams of space
so that no matter how much
life betrays your heart
you could read the words that
begin with

"These are the voyages[3]"
and also

*"To love the journey is
to accept no such end[4]"*

and would thus always be able
to find your way home.

This inheritance from my father
is perhaps the only riches I have
to give you.

I will write new fables
for the future.

(Never forget
there are few heroes in
your story, only humans
who continue on.)

Theology may fail you
and the measure of our
scientific understanding
is limited,
but the myths and legends
you were steeped in since
birth will continue enlarging as
you grow, until the monsters tower

---

[3] Star Trek TNG, "Encounter at Farpoint."
[4] Brandon Sanderson, Oathbringer (The Stormlight Archive, #3).

over all you
can build and the dragon breathes
heat into
your soul.

(Few stories are wholly factual.
find the truth within them,
and your roots will pull
water from
whatever ground
in which you are planted.)

ELOCUTION

Your words washed
over me
and I was pulled in, captured.

For a moment I was in
a place both familiar and
strange.

I saw you, I saw
through
your eyes.

Your words were a map
guiding a path between
your perspective
and my own.

I was caught up,
ripped from life's daily
distractions and pains.

I floated for a while above the sky.

And then my feet became heavy.
They weighed a thousand pounds!

So back to the ground, I fell, and
the earth was enough to hold me.

I have discovered that,
for this day,
what I have is sufficient,

as you

shared grace from
your share, and
my feet are not heavy,
they are planted,
and I am not floating,
I am rejoicing

and
my belly is full
and
my heart is quiet.

Did you know that
you mastered that
sorcery?

The spell to
refresh a soul?

To pour your
words through my
ears and eyes,
until I overflowed
and could
not resist the
weight of
that triumph?

If it has been a while
since I reminded you of your
power, let
me do so
now.

ILLUMINATION

I have seen the light.
The glare was too intense to view
for long,
but in the moment before I
blinked,
I knew the true nature of man.

In the thickest mud

there is glory there

  In the clearest water
  there is glory there

  In the blood of sacrifice
  there is glory there

  In the breath of peace
  there is glory there

  In the hottest flames
  there is glory there

I blinked, and then my eyes
refocused,
but for a second, I transcended
and knew the true nature of the
world.

There is nothing more sacred than
dirt.

If there is "my way"
there also must be "your way"
and if there is hope for us on this
dying rock,
may our ways intersect, even if
only for

  a shared meal

  a shared story

  a shared song

  a shared laugh

  a shared outburst.

In that place of crossings
we will know the light—it will be
too bright
to behold for long.

But before we blink,
we may transcend
and learn the true measure of
time.

Let us meet there, and
dance a wild caper,
one which knows no
striving or fear.

Let us step into
our true forms.

I will meet you there.

THE WITCH'S END

My snacks spoiled, spilled out on the leather, baked in the sun. My blood had dripped from the steering wheel and dried into rust on the floorboards. I do not remember; others told me this story. I do recall the sharp words that woke me.

I was told that I must have sinned to face such a fate, as I was not healed. The miracle child's blessing had passed. The voice did not call me; I could not remember my name. My memory grew holes; my stories were in tatters as my faith fell away like discarded wrapping paper.

Thus ended the witch, smote by God, condemned to wander the earth nameless and weak and afraid, stripped of her powers, performing penance for the sins that bred me and shaped me, the sins that I committed, the death I had willed.

One night, as I reclined on the couch in my mother's library, I saw the veil between worlds. It was so thin—I wanted to reach out and grasp the light I could see in the corner of my eyes and slip into a cold eternity. I cannot tell you why I chose to stay. Perhaps I believed there were fates left for me to craft, days when I would dance to bring the rains again.

I did not walk again because of the power of God; I did not rise from my wheelchair in another miracle. I walked because it was the end of that cycle of suffering. There have been many more. But I hid this truth and let myself be trotted out as a "witness" as I told of how I was set free once I had repented for the errors of my ways. I learned to lie well. I coated my aching bones in thick muscle and ran as many miles as it would take before the cycle began again. I waited through the years, taking shallow breaths and never resting too long in one place. (This is a terrible testimony; it will not carry over a key change; it will not fit before offertory—it is a poor hymn.)

It took many tries to find faith again. It took many years to understand that what I had lost was faith in myself.

This is my faith, now: The voice that called to me, called to me by name, did not lie. It was the first voice that spoke to me the truth. Because of that voice, I knew to hear you when you told me my name. And I have yet endured.

This is also my faith now:

A swerve, a veer, a skid, a crash
  the witch did not burn

Harsh lights, fluids dripping, needles pressing, blood pooling
  the witch did not float

Broken skin, torn nerves, crushed bones, changed countenance
  the witch did bleed

Sharp wit, firm will, dark nights, loud laments
  the witch was marked

I held my soul firmly in my flesh in the night before waking you. I forgot old spells and lost touch with the monsters of the deep. I have recalled entire centuries, but still wove my path through history enough times that the patterns became muddy and I could create nothing with my hands or words or tones but that which is right here before you. I did eventually remember my name. My heart is weak. I cannot run. But I lied—I did not end.

Let's set out on the drive again. I'll plan a more straightforward path, and you'll keep keener eyes on the road. We'll rest after a while; we should take our time. You pick the direction. I will be fine—sitting here beside you, sipping hot tea to moisten my tongue—no matter where we go. I didn't pack a bag. We'll find what we need when we get there.

IT IS SO BRIEF

And here is the moment
when I look upon all
I have traversed and
what I have done.

I am so small
and all I have wrought
is never enough.

I am not an optimist
so my "silver lining"
is a rather
dulled pewter.

But I am still here, yes?
Still breathing?
Still?

I will assume there is time
left for my undertaking.

DANCING

I stepped into the water
with heavy feet.
The sky was overcast,
the waves crashing
past my knees.

The wind caught my
arms and raised them high.
I stretched toward
the moon and
began the dance.

My steps beat the drum
within the heart of the earth,
the creatures of the deep
whirled along beside me.

Each step I took
resounded
with a tone that
penetrated
the watery abyss.

I danced for the living, for
the dying, for the ill
I danced for the wanderers
I am dancing still.

This step...

    boom!
is for the ceaseless fatiguing
winds.

This step...

    boom!
is for when the salt seeps
through your skin.

This step...

    boom!
is for the rains to sooth the
dryness.

This step...

    boom!
is for the nights so sleepless.

I grasped the roots of the deep
and wrapped the waves around
me.

I swallowed the ocean whole and
became its choppy rhythms.

Regretting the taking,
I spilled the water—
filling the basins deep,
past the brim.

Seaweed grows from my
limbs, rooted in my veins.
I walk the ocean still;
my heavy feet dance on.

This step...

>   *boom!*
resounds for the lost ones.

This step...

>   *boom!*
cries out for the aged ones.

This step...

>   *boom!*
is for the ones who fear.

Weep a million tears
and join me in the ocean!
Let the breaking of the
waves bring the dance
from deep within you.
Stretch your hands
to the moon
and feel your weight
sink in the sand.

My sister will sing
the song
to bring
the winds.

The winds will
flow and
sweep
and bring
the rain

and we will
join the

>   *beating*

>   *pounding*

>   *crashing*

>   *booming*
as your soul
joins the dance!

Together, we

>   *sing in voices sweet*

Together, we

>   *move with heavy feet*

Together, we

    bring the waves
    bring the winds
    bring the rains

All together...

    boom!

The soul of the Earth
is dancing!

BENEDICTION

Or, All I Ever Needed to Know I Learned in a Space Ship

I was born in the future. There, I have seen two suns pull twenty worlds into orbit; I have measured the light from the last of the stars to blink out in eternal darkness; I have felt a black hole inhale all I've ever known and loved. I am stuck in a loop of time, with temporal energies caking my hands, and with all the new worlds I have inhabited, I cannot definitively say I have a soul. But I will burn up this star to reach you, to come close enough to you that we might extinguish the air between our hands, our lips; skin to skin we will stand as the storm rages, and when we part, we will each carry sand on the bottom of our shoes.

The future is the past, but I was born as a preacher, a preacher who wanders planet-side and tries to speak for the living after mourning the dead. Whether we send the bodies into space or bury them deep in the ground or burn them to ashes or plant them with trees, they will never feel the cold or warmth or searing heat. The temperature variance is for us, those who travel in our tin cans through silent voids, as it makes us feel more human despite how far removed we are from the earth.

We cannot learn who we are from the dead alone, but we must begin there. Do you believe you have thought new thoughts or prayed new prayers?

No one knows what is in one's own heart or mind. We cannot easily observe all the viscous fluids traveling through one's own systems nor follow a thought as it proceeds by electrical impulses from this point in the brain to that one (without specialized equipment). You cannot see the idea that rips you from your previous self to float in the ether for a while until you descend into your next configuration.

No one knows who they will be by the time they die. When you are young, you are too close to the vastness of your birth to have a proper perspective on the size of all else. As you age, your mind is pulled to every nick and crevice of time, even as time marks itself on you. By the time death is something you have experienced, not just witnessed, you will be forever changed in a fraction of an instant and cannot tell those left behind what it is like.

So then, chase the shadows, the light, the wind. Become the moon, the sun, the stars. Float the streams, the creeks, the rivers. Descend to the depths of the ocean until you can no longer breathe, and after resurfacing, flee the confines of gravity until your home is a distant speck in the dark. Through all of these travels, you will remain yourself. You see, even the far reaches of space contain cosmic dust, and we, of course, are forever returning to the dust of the earth as we begin the process of expiring shortly after birth. These truths give me comfort, as regardless of how far we roam from our home, we will likely still need to bathe when we get there, and thus, the Earth will be forever joined with the depths of the unknown as we exfoliate.

Coat yourself in soapy suds, in water, in salts, in oils; roll in the mud and let it cake in the sun, rinse it off, and begin again. You will lose skin cells while building a memory that tells you what I mean when I say you may dissolve into the firmament, but you will still be yourself.

I have flown apart countless times, been destroyed in the void, rendered impotent, and reformed again to sit in this chair and pen these pages. Did you know? Have you spent your years running and turning and changing and reinventing? Or did you discover this truth early and find contentment?

Did you know?

I do not know your name, only your face, only your appearance I have seen through the filters in my mind, and for us to share this moment, I have to abandon the molds in which I baked my thoughts. I have to trust you to know me, despite me, to feel that my heart pounds out a cadence to give purpose to my cold words, to allow me to speak, to let me listen.

It is, I fear, too much responsibility for any one person, but it is the world we are given.

I am no hero nor villain—just one who survived. But I stand here, the size that I am—unafraid.

I didn't know, but I am beginning to see. Here is my tale for the living, for this living life, for my life, for I have few answers and more confusion, but I have learned to love the questions. I was born in the future but will die in the past. In that moment, before I end what I am and become what is next, I will know my true size and live what I preach.

Or perhaps I won't. But it is enough, I think, to be myself, even now, even with all I don't know. What else could I be?

This is my sermon. It's not in three parts, and I think I forgot the takeaways, the charges to action, the calls to the altar, but I've mixed enough metaphors for one day, for one lyrical examination of the queries that drive me.

Or perhaps not.

Let us bow our heads and tread boldly into the center of the questions that we might ask, throw away insignificance so we might deduce what truly happened, clean time's refuse from underneath our fingernails, and lift our eyes from our puny human existence long enough to consider the bright, tiny speck we are in the cosmos. And that is what I mean when I say, "Amen."

This gap is for you.

Who do you think you are?

You didn't think
I would end with
transcendence,
did you?

It is only a start.

OF **CASTLES BUILT** & SELDOM **DISMANTLED**

NAME CHANGE

I began again at Jacob's well. There,
I heard the words which perforated
my principles
and it was at this place I chose to forgive.

Not for you, for me.

Now I claim my birthright:
to speak being into the voids.

Not for me, for you.

A LETTER TO MY GRANDMOTHERS NAMED MARIE

I know of bits and pieces of you, starved for tales of truth, lost in daydreams full of cotton-blended wishes, so unlike the true weaves that barely held us together. I know the names given to you, but not those torn from you before you even reached the age to choose monikers that would forever remain solely your own. You were barely an adolescent, still a child.

Is it from you that I have inherited the knowing, the never forgetting, the pre-born awareness that I would never be safe in the way others were safe? Was my knowing all my own, the making of the years I lived, or did something of your long days and longer nights tag your genes so that I would know when they descended down to me? *They* always knew. *Homewrecker in the making, sweet Jezebel, ripe for the taking*, they crooned their false promises of protection, but the words they spoke over my head still fell to my feet and tripped me up time and again.

My daughter knows. I wish I could wrap her in blankets and hide her somewhere safe, but where would that be? Surely not the closets, the pantries. Surely not the hallways, the altars.

I chose to marry, but I must wonder if you were offered the same, for all you were offered the catechism and rites so your names could be remade; you were named Marie; you were never named Marie.

My father once told me that I was Coyote's child. I asked him what he meant, and he tried to sketch Coyote's likeness with his words. But he kept drawing a line, then erasing it; drawing a line, erasing, and I felt as if I was trying to connect the stars to make constellations in someone else's sky. He grew tired, and his mouth pressed thin, and said perhaps he had forgotten what Coyote looked like or maybe it had all been a dream or maybe he just made it up. I wouldn't say I like it when stories end that way.

They tell me they can see your wildness, that I've never quite fit in the neat and tidy places, that my laugh is unmistakable, that my eyes are unnerving, that my voice is strangely melodic. They tell me I make them afraid, intimidated, insecure; they say I am temptation; I wear my physicality plainly. Did you know my humor is broken? Did you know I do not do well waiting quietly for my turn? I do not know which of you gave me what, but the cornucopia of mismatched heirlooms that are my birthright were often bitter in taste and unwieldy to store. I didn't learn how to season and savor until later.

How did your laugh sound?

We're getting ready to leave—hiding, I mean. I don't even know where to begin. What do I bring? But I wanted you to hear me, to hear my prayers to you, to breathe the smoke I've lifted for you, to see the hair I've shorn for you, that I've braided for you. I've never forgotten you for all I don't know.

We'll be leaving the shadows, for all I prefer how they cling and follow me as I slip in and out of rooms you would never have been allowed to see. I know that I'll have to learn new rhythms and songs, but I'll likely continue the practice of changing my skins—am I here to answer your prayers? Even so, I won't forget how to evade. Just in case.

But I promised you, didn't I, that I would try? Will you stay with me, here, while I try?

SCENE NOTES FOR THE CHORUS

Pardon me, I need a moment in which we forgo the illusions intrinsic
to this design, and speak plainly. You may not understand *literally*
everything I am sharing, but that is all right; knowledge is relations, not
merely the absorption of an objective elucidation of facts. You should
know that for me, I might as well be naked.

You won't all fit in my bedroom or my couch, where I normally reside
when I'm this tired. So, pretend you're there with me, and we're all
uncomfortably close. We've set the scene, and I've taken the stage. I
tried to hire a different player—she'd be taller, willowy, less ambiguous,
distinctly something or another. Her skin would be uniform in tone.
She wouldn't be breaking out in hives or have stomach bloat or inflamed
joints. She would be confident but demure, gentle-toned and secure,
never awkward or misplaced. But we only have the budget for me.

For this work, I must take down the masks. Naked or adorned is
immaterial, but the memories stored in my muscles and fascia and all
my connective tissue give me *The Face*. The *Public* Face, more specifically,
to go with the confident poise honed years ago at the ballet barre. But
that won't work here. Pardon me for a moment, if you will, while I strip
myself bare.

Will you breathe with me? Send your shoulders away from your ears,
relax your arms, and: *Breathe in two, three, four, hold, two, three, four,*
breathe out two, three four
hold, two, three, four
and again
and again.

There. Do you feel the way your muscles have shifted? Touch your
cheeks. Feel their looseness? That's the face I wear at home. Or a near
approximation.

NUMBER OF MAN

6.

My feet hurt this morning,
but I could feel them
and thus, I could balance all right.

I was afraid this afternoon,
and so I made tea, sat in
the sun, and focused on my
breathing.

5.

When disease set in, I knew it was
time to face the truth of who I am.

I am all of these things:
sacred, mundane, profane.

Horrible and beautiful and plain.
You are these things as well.

4.

You may hear these words and
wonder,
"Is that all there is to her,
such a cynical view?"

And in response, I would ask:
what is more holy, more
sacrosanct, than being an animal
who looks at the sky and
wonders if there is a God,
and when given no measurable
proof,
continues to build
and achieve and work to
add meaning, to form
moats carved from sand
to protect a castle which
cannot outlast the tides?

I can think of nothing,
except for such an animal
who faces its small stature
and answers the questions
born of pain
with joy.

3.

Recently, I was explaining to a
friend who uses a wheelchair
how I knew that she suffered in
ways I don't understand.

She interrupted me and did not let
me continue.

She told me that is something
able-bodied people say to
one another, and instead, I should
take as much empathy as I need
when I suffer
and give as much empathy as I
have to give.

I had never been given a similar
scripture.

I was still waiting for my
miraculous healing,
to prove to myself that I was

worthy of care.

I had made her into my
inspiration,
and I knew then
how much she had to hate that.

She never volunteered.

2.

The week after the funeral, I went
to a new Sunday school
and my teacher introduced me as
the girl whose
father just died, and from that
moment on, everything I achieved
was compared to his slow slip into
death.

"Isn't she inspirational?" they
would say,
as I was trotted out
like a show pony,
at the moments in the story in
which someone needed a good cry,
after the slow songs
but before the offering.

"See how much she has
overcome?"
they would say,
when all I did was show up
just like everyone else.

1.

I never asked to be your fucking
inspiration.

The framework of all I would and
could and will be
was measured out and counted:
the first time I was struck
the first time I was violated
the first time I cried out to a cold
and empty night.

Few saw that such things were
merely part of the
dust from which I am formed.

BLUE-VEIN SOCIETY

I, of the first generation who may pass in the manner to which you are accustomed, reject my share of the full fruits of the many years of breeding that favored minimal pigmentation.

My father learned to destroy himself from generations before him and taught me the craft of immolation of the soul through strength of will and denial of self. It took many years before I could reject this tradition. I am a specter in my lineage, a ghost of privilege able to slide into the room as the other or the default at will. I was taught my people's stories out of context, to pray to a God who only wanted my brightness, to be quiet and behave, and thus to become a pillar holding up the very hatred that made me.

I was unwanted, rejected, nameless, and for a long time I could not exceed the identity of fragility I was willed, for whenever I attained a measure of freedom another player would arise to shatter the illusion of my strength. Violation is an oft-used tool to ensure that we remember our places. Rape is not sex—it is war.

I was not born a slave, and therefore, I cannot judge those who had recently escaped, developed a strategy to attain what could be gained, and discarded an entire people—themselves—to forget trauma. But I do judge my time. I do reject my membership in the blue-vein society. I refuse to ask anyone to stand just to the side while we take the family picture. I will not maintain the culture which kept me fragile. I do not care if this means only inhabiting the places in between. I have learned to thrive in the void.

Perhaps you would be willing to hear my words if I were to assume a more recognized position for one of my stations—on my back or on my knees. But I am not so easily packaged and consumed.

I speak the words that will lodge in your craw.

Thus, this is my quest, my question—to do what has yet to be done in my family, to be indeed free from slavery, to destroy the system designed to create victims or victors but never people of many facets, people allowed to hold firm, to know their power, to wield their magic.

And so I wander in the wilderness. Forty years circling the same mountain. Forty generations of penance for the sins that bred me. Forty centuries of meeting my ancestors. Forty millennia of learning to follow those called to lead. Forever to remember my name and what it means to live within and outside of my skin, what it means to recognize that though I have scars in the deepest of places, I am indestructible.

An instant to repent for my ignorance.

A lifetime as yet untold to learn a new way, and to love all of me, so that I may gaze past my own navel to look you in the eyes and see you as you say you are.

Eternity to cry out with the voices that called to me. To sing out a true song, to speak true tales, to pray true prayers. To learn to do justice, as my brother has taught me. I acknowledge the ugly parts of me, the angry parts, the parts that never left that bed, that closet, that room, that altar, the parts that stopped feeling when I faced situations in which no one was right, and everyone had blood on their hands.

I have returned to my childhood to begin growing again as one who is strong and does not need anyone to diminish themselves so that I may feel safe. So when I sing out, it is still the song of a child, a simple melody, perhaps out of key. Still, I will sing out loudly and call with all who will join as we work to dismantle our inheritance of false freedom in order to live, breathe, grow, stretch, bend, break, heal, remember, return, and follow. To hold fast to one another. To hold fast to a peace born of justice and to resist the onslaught of those who consume their fear in many flavors.

To those who resist the truth, resist freedom, to those who claim ignorance as a birthright in place of your real name, to those who destroy the hope of others so that you may feel well armed and righteous, know that we are many who hold the line at this sacred place. We will not be defeated. You will not pass.

SELAH

I empathize with parents who put their toddlers on leashes—there was no way mine would have stood for such treatment. No, she was facing me with a set jaw, a glint in her eyes, and an unbending spine from the moment she could stand and face me.

It's how I knew she was mine.

While ultimately endearing, this fearlessness and the ability to thwart all strategic planning and defensive tactics in mere seconds made bath time a nightly torture for her parents. The nights we escaped a drenched bathroom, a busted lip (sometimes hers, usually mine), or other damage to our home or persons were timidly celebrated with cheap wine once we convinced the child to sleep. Or at least, to *pretend* to sleep.

Thus, we began each bath by reciting together the bath-time rules. In doing this, I hoped they would burn into her psyche, and we would avoid needing the first-aid kit before bedtime. I have my version of the rules, the proper version, of course, in that they are the originals and predate my child's development of critical-thinking skills. However, I will end this preamble with a recitation of my child's version, told to me one night when she was old enough to repeat the nightly liturgy without (too much) prompting.

"Tell me, what are the rules about bath time?" I said. "The first rule is…"

Lower lip pulled in with her teeth, eyes cast over her shoulder as she thought.

"The first rule is don't touch the knob because I will make the water really hot or really cold and then cry about it."

"Right. Next?"

"Don't get water on the floor or all over Mommy," she giggled.

"Right. Very important, that one. And the last?"

A slight pause. I could see her grasp for the words, and then a happy smile bloomed as she remembered. "I know! The last one is, *dommit, child, sit on your bottom!*"

"Ahem," I uttered while attempting to control chagrined laughter. "Are you sure that's how the last one goes?"

"Well, mommy, I don't think it's how it's *supposed* to go. But that's the way you always say it!"

She collapsed to the floor in giggles. I was convinced of my earlier opinion, expressed to the nurses at the hospital who helped us load the new baby and all of the new-baby accoutrements into the car, that perhaps I should not have been allowed to procreate.

"Well, it's a bit late now, dear! Don't worry about it. You'll be fine," they replied, cheerfully waving as we drove off.

As I am sitting here writing this story with all of my limbs intact and the loud sounds of a teenager in her room bossing her friends around with an eagerness that makes me both cringe and fill with pride, I suppose I can affirm that we *are* fine.

But it was a narrow escape, there for a bit.

We were of the chosen parents given a wiggly newborn who not only interrupted our lives in all the manners that newborns do but a wiggly newborn who also came with colic. If you have not had a baby with colic, I do not want to hear about how your baby also cried at times, and it was tough for you. If you have—if perhaps right now you are attempting to read these words while being kept from sleep and sanity in a manner forced upon you with such tenacity that you are hiding in the darkest recesses of your psyche from the piercing, shrill cries that seem to last every minute of every day for years on end—if we meet in person, just let me know. I will buy you a drink, no questions asked.

She cried for what seemed like forever. I knew I was not of the type to bond quickly with my child, and the colic did not ease this process. I quickly became despondent. I could do nothing to calm my baby, which seemed to prove my earlier fears that I should never have become a mother.

One night, in what was either a few weeks or many long ages after her birth (the early months aren't so good for the telling of time), I held her desperately in my arms. I had long given up singing and rocking and walking and warm cloths and cool ones and lavender and pleading with whatever deities might hear me when I began to fill with the rage I had feared ever since I saw it course through my father's face.

I wanted nothing more than to shake her, to hit her, to do anything to make this stop. I am ashamed that this is true, but I promised that I would not lie—not even to you.

Perhaps my husband sensed my precarious state, perhaps I cried out unknowingly. Thankfully, he intervened with the tiny terror at least an hour before his scheduled shift, leaving me to flee before I could cause any harm.

I don't remember what I did next or where I was. I only remember the insides of my mind. I once lived in fear of my parents' quick tempers and cruel words. I recalled promising myself that I would never treat my child in the same manner. And in that bit of time, somewhere between a single instant or a lifetime, I was filled with stark clarity; I could do nothing to prevent my descent into becoming the abuser without willingly facing my darkness—which meant witnessing the scars on my body and my mind and treating the wounds that never healed, preferably with professional assistance.

Though I thought I had faced this before, the past times of brokenness were nothing on that moment. If you know the fear that you will damage your children in the ways you were harmed, you know the dark night of the soul I walked through that evening.

If you don't, I am so glad.

This was not a single moment that changed all. It was the first of many moments in which I chose to walk away, to face my sins, to repent, and turn back to my family. I wish I could say that I never failed in this daily practice. I wish I could tell you that my child has never heard me raise my voice or seen me lose my temper.

I can say that I have never hit her, violated her, implied I never wanted her, or told her she ruined my life and should have never been born. My family did not set the bar too high for me to surpass it.

But I have most certainly failed her at times.

That night, when I faced the impossibly fierce rage against the baby I was supposed to protect and love, I decided that while I was unlikely to be a perfect mother or even a particularly nurturing mother, I did have the power to be an honest mother. I would always own up to my mistakes. I would show her where I went wrong and what I had to do to correct my course. I would never fear telling her the stories that made me who I was so she would grow up knowing why her life was hers from the beginning. And I would indeed never fear asking for help if, at any moment, my demons caused risk to my child.

A few weeks after that night, she smiled at me for the first time. At that moment, I believed that someday we might be fine.

A few years ago, she told me that I can be scary.

"Scary like I would hurt you?" I asked.

She thought. "No, more, well, scary like you always know what I'm doing, and you're going to make me look at the truth. Sometimes, you made me *so mad* because I knew that you would just stand there and wait for me to do what I should no matter what. You can wait forever. But now, you're not as scary. It's probably because I'm almost as tall as you."

"Whatever," I responded. "You'll never be taller than me. Am I still your favorite mommy-monster?"

She gave a big smile as she snuggled close. "The best mommy-monster. If anybody tried to hurt me, I know you'd be way more scary to them. You're like, well, a stone wall around me that will never move. You'll always keep me safe."

My heart warmed and broke at the same time. I have always hated when movie parents tell their children that they will always be there for them. It is foreboding. It never ends well.

I told her the truth. That while I would do my best mommy-monster act if anyone tried to hurt her, even if I might hurt her, I am only so big. There are many things much bigger than I, for all I like to pretend that I got to grow up to be tall.

She looked me deep in the eyes and said, "You mean, like, death?"

"I do mean, like, death—and other things. You know I will always do my best, and so will your daddy. But we are no bigger than human."

My daughter has always been wiser than I. My wisdom was forged from my own stubborn pride and refusal to quit; hers was born into her like magic.

The first time she had to mourn, truly mourn, that was a day. Our community was small and gossiped in the way that small communities do. Our friend was well-loved, and I knew I could not protect my child from hearing what happened. And so I told her. There is nothing like telling your eight-year-old that her second mother was killed by her husband, and thus, their son—her chosen brother—was moving away. Nothing like holding her while her soul shattered for the first time as she mourned the whole family. Nothing like her crying with me night after night for months as she feared I would die and leave her forever, as my health was beginning to diminish, and she was sure that autoimmune diseases were just like bullets.

I had already prepared her for facing death as best as I could. By the time I was an adult, I had been to more than a dozen funerals. They were more familiar to me than weddings. And so I never, ever promised that I could keep all bad things from happening or that I would never leave her. I told her I hoped I would beat her to dying and that all parents ultimately hoped that, as no parent would want to outlive their child.

I started small.

Though we told everyone that we had strict rules against electronic toys for our daughter, that was the first family rule everyone ignored. And so, on her first birthday, we were the proud recipients of a Chicken-Dance Elmo.

I have never hated anything or anyone[5] more than that toy. Of course, my daughter grew to love him and would dance along with Chicken-Dance Elmo repeatedly (she was rather adorable, despite my ire against her dancing muse). Of course, the batteries seemed magically charmed never to run out, and Chicken-Dance Elmo lived with us nigh on forever.

On the day the batteries finally died—there was no way I was replacing them—I held my somber child as I told her that all things pass. We hosted a small funeral, complete with a burial for Chicken-Dance Elmo. She told me I had to give a "yew-low-gee" (she asked her Mima about the proper way to do funerals). I spoke a few dignified and surprisingly poignant words as we all felt the varying feelings such days bring to the surface.

On the day I told my child what happened to our beautiful friend, after crying for a while in the arms of her father, she looked up at me and asked, "Is she in heaven?"

"You know, I believe that she endures somewhere, in some way," I answered, "though I will not tell you if that is definitively true. You will find your own faith, even in this."

She sat in quiet for a long time with her head bowed. And then, a small smile broke through the dark visage of her face. It was a timid smile, a smile that had mourned, and nothing had ever hurt more than seeing the evidence that my child was now familiar with violence and death. She looked up at me.

"I think she is in heaven. I think she's up there with Chicken-Dance Elmo and your daddy. I bet she's making everyone up there laugh and giving them a second helping at dinner."

---

[5] If I'm being honest, there are a few players on the American political stage whose behavior render this statement entirely false.

Years later, her smiles became braver again, if a bit snarkier than before. Her humor developed a dark twist. She has never stopped trying to take care of me and protect me from all things, and I often remind her that she is no bigger than human and none of us are in control.

There was nothing like facing the fear of having her. Not of birthing her—pain and I were old friends, and I knew I would endure—but having and keeping her. I knew that night, as I promised that I would do all I could not only to protect her but to prepare for the days when I could not protect my baby, that I would never be in control again. I would always be at the mercy of my progeny.

For years, I sat next to Selah in time-outs as she sobbed and tearfully told me how she didn't mean it and she would do better. There was no need to yell or spank. One raised eyebrow, and she was off to the corner with a broken soul; we held the pieces for her while she knit her heart back together.

It worked for us.

One night, her father wasn't nearby for the time-out breakdown, and Selah refused consolation. Desperate to provide some comfort and perhaps a relevant moralizing story, I told her a tale of tripping over a laundry basket and fuming about it until her dad had laughed at me so long that I had to join in. My daughter erupted in giggles so fierce that she nearly choked, and then she climbed into my lap.

"Mama, I bet you looked really silly," she said. And though I had always hated being the object of mockery, the moment I saw the relief from her sorrow and a burgeoning awareness that even mommy-monsters can't be perfect all of the time, I knew I would tell her every embarrassing tale if only she knew I never wanted her to be anything other than the best human she could be.

This is why, in a collection of tales about facing the terrible things of life, and despite the literary world's general prejudice against light verse, I have attempted to make you laugh.

Laughter is the best rebellion against death.

Should you not find me to be funny, it is all right. You may find your joy somewhere.

RISE

When faced with incomprehensible tragedy, it is easy to retreat. It is easier to sleep in the shadow of the suffering around us than it is to remain awake with eyes that perceive.

Every generation has seen cities burn and mothers lose their children and fathers drift homeless and broken. Every age is heralded with weeping and steeped in grief. War and chaos saturate every eon. There has never been a life untouched by sorrow in some measure.

We question if the sky is falling, wonder if we will be the last to walk on this earth. Surely, no one has lived to see the violence that marks our age. And we ask these questions of God, of one another, or of ourselves, as all those who breathe and speak have always done. We hold our babies close and fear the approaching night.

It is painful to say there is no safe place on this earth. Sorrow can find you in wars, in floods, in storms, in the quiet approaching sleep of cancer, the instantaneous end of a bullet. In our world there dwells relentless death.

We say, let us hide in our caves or castles, our cottages or our monasteries, or in our homes, all barely lit to dampen the night. We will surround ourselves with safeness, with safe feelings and safe words, and no harm will come to us.

But I have seen cities burn and bow down in the face of storms; I have seen children taken from their mothers, fathers torn from their families, so many lost in the embers of illness and anger. I have seen this in wealthy, lonely homes and in places so poor if you give a child a pair of shoes, they won't wear them out of fear of having them.

There is no safe place.

For years, the things I have seen chased me down in my sleep. I dreamt the death of all I love over and over for ages without end.

It is easy to give platitudes, to pour verses over wounds in those around us whom we cannot heal, whose wounds we can't even comprehend. And then, our consciences mollified, we go back to sleep.

But I say, rise.

Rise and see. Rise and see and weep, for all is broken. Let the grief change you and shape you. Question the meaning of it all and let that question keep you up at night. Violence inhabits our culture from grief that we never wept.

Rise and wonder, what difference could you possibly make? Paint pictures that will anger you because you don't understand how anyone could paint in the face of tragedy. Fiddle while cities burn and let the songs permeate your soul and change who you are, and then your notes may find their meaning. Tell the stories you wish you could forget. Hold one another close. Mourn with those who mourn.

Rise.

There will be another day, a day when there is peace and the grief will be less sharp against your skin, and on that day, you will want to sleep. Rise. Open your eyes and create, bring your dreams into the day, and let the bright sun saturate the dreamscapes until you can barely see for their brightness. Fear the power of your dreams, and then run into the worlds you have built with your whole heart.

Rise. Dream while awake. See what beauty your hands can make and think on these things.

Keep your dreams. Keep your hope. Guard your love fiercely; when all else is gone, love may remain.

I have seen sorrow and yet stay awake.

My grief is endless, but my hope endures.

How can this be?

Rise and seek.

REVELATIONS

As Taught to Me by My Oldest Friend

The years do not set us down straight paths.

Rather,
life is in the
bending
winding
curving
and reshaping.

When the world ends,
 we should
   dance and
   laugh and
   drink and
 sing out over
the
dying embers

and know that for a time
we were rooted in
this place,
and it was good.

FINAL INTERLUDE

Gather your things,
shift in your seat,
stretch your legs.

We have reached an end.
The end? Doubtful.

I am sure I will
have more to say
when we meet again.

(I hope I live longer than this.)

TOMORROW

If you are inside, is there a window nearby? If so, do me a favor and transport yourself to it however you are able, open it, and turn your senses to the outside. If you can't, I understand. You can imagine this bit if needed.

If you are outside, you're already there.

You may be surrounded by trees, grass, a well-trimmed lawn. You may be immersed in city streets, tall buildings, stop signs. You may smell mountains, oceans, streams, or factories. You may hear a ship deck or a prison yard or the beeping of a heart monitor. You may see the earth far, far below you. You may be aware of nothing but the dead of night. Regardless of your surroundings, take a moment and thoroughly perceive it. Know your size, your perspective, the angles around you, the direction the wind blows (if there is wind, where you are).

That's tomorrow. Regardless of what happens to you, those things will still be. Or, perhaps, will be. Change happens. All things die. But no matter how many breaths you have left to breathe, no matter how many days you have left to be aware of where you are, no matter—you will be outlived.

Now, rest your eyes. Take a deep breath and hold it.

Exhale.

And again.

And again.

And once more.

And now. Open your senses wide. Breathe naturally. Feel the heaviness of your bones and the temperature of the air on your skin.

That's tomorrow. It is much the same as today, except for all we cannot see, which is mostly everything.

You have no idea. Neither do I. It's a fine thing not to know, for though I will never be one to tell you that there are only adventures to come, I will tell you that many things will happen, and you will survive them as long as you can.

It doesn't always feel like enough. Sometimes, you may take stock of all you have done, built, held, kissed, consumed, and squashed, and you ache with the knowledge of the fleeting nature of things. Remember all you knew when we began. Observe it—it's not so grand.

Here for an instant. A bare second in cosmic time, yet how many questions have you had time to ask? How many hands have you grasped?

When your end comes, do me a favor: As you are there, facing your last bits of time in the world that is now, like a child standing on the beach as the sun falls into the ocean and the moon rises to bring a new tide, give your castle of sand a good, swift, kick for me.

You've built enough.

It's a good way to go.

But before that day comes, you have *now*. Tomorrow will only be another *now*. Now, what do you have? Now, who do you think you are? Now, where will you go next?

You have no idea. Neither do I. Oh, it is terrifying, of course. I do understand that you are afraid. And we all think we would be so much better if only we could bend the fates to our will.

(Even with all I have done, I have never done such a thing as that.)

But would we be... better?

You may as well rest for a while. Who knows what strength you will need for the journey? Don't forget to pack sustenance. Drink plenty of water and sleep when you are able. You may learn to find what you need wherever you are.

What's next for me? I think I am ready to jump into the unknown despite the long hike to reach this place.

Would you like to jump with me?

Don't worry. I'll go first.

But I can't swim so well—metaphorically or otherwise—so don't hold onto the cliff too long after you see me begin the fall. Please?

I should warn you, the water is quite cold—but clear, and the drop only lasts a moment.

How about now?

Now?

Now.

HOLOMETABOLISM

Who am I before? I think I am solid and unmoving, encasing my limbs in a fixed material to make a strong base for the statue entitled "This Should Have Been Me." I cannot quite capture the likeness. But this stillness is not a bad place to begin; all I need to do now is find a branch that can hold my weight and affix myself firmly.

I do not know how I know it is time, but I do, almost like a craving deep within for something I have never taken in. I stuff myself full of greens—I will need more calories and nutrients than I have stored. I shed my skin five times, molting until I am raw and unprotected. I press all my being outward to allow for a hard casing to form around me. Slowly, I squeeze my whole self through my gastric system. Deep inhales, shaky gasps, as the muscles around my lungs dissolve. How do you breathe while digesting yourself?

I think I just choked on my spleen.

I am impatient, so in the last moment, before my eyes are devoured, I rip deep past my navel into my belly to see the process more closely. Upon further consideration, this more profound knowledge of the process is not helpful, and I close my eyes tightly in hopes of forgetting what I have seen. (I have never been able to leave things well enough alone.)

Curling inward as I continue to ooze, my brain meets my knees as I fold into a fetal figure, and then my bones give way. I struggle to hold the template of what I might become in my pineal eye while allowing it to change and shift even as I do. I am surprised by the emotions—my anger seeps from my intestines, my fear from my shins, joy from my tongue, love from my breast, pleasure from my sex, and now nothing is compartmentalized as I am permeated by all I once locked down deep within me. I am only sensation.

The stew that is me thumps with each rapid beat of my heart. In this moment, I am nothing that I was nor that I will be. This instant seems

to last for all of time, for how do I know how long this is taking? I cannot
check the time on my phone. If I were a moth, this process would only
take a few weeks. For a while, all I feel is that, for once, I am taking
up as much space as I need, and every part of me is warm. I consider
remaining shapeless to avoid the work ahead. But I need new fingers to
scratch the itch on my new back. I only take a brief respite.

I try not to think of those who fail mid-transition. Forms forever held
in chrysalises that never achieve their potential. Should I calcify in this
state, will you dissect me so that you may learn where I went wrong?

When I am done, I will need to cut myself free. I should have sharpened
my teeth.

I try to capture a memory of becoming new, but I cannot yet perceive,
and my language is yet to return. My limbs stretch in supple form, ready
to tear at my cocoon with uncalloused hands. My heart beats wildly; I am
not prepared to leave; I do not know what I will sound like; I do not know
if I will recognize myself when I pass by a mirror, but I am convulsing
with a contraction of my skin and with one great, violent surge I break
open.

The air smells of sweat and new life—of regurgitation. New sinew
holds new muscles to my joints, and the old casing falls to the ground.
Somehow, I find myself rooted on feet with new toes. I open new eyes. I
am still nearsighted. Would you hand me my glasses and my cane? I am a
little unsteady.

I am going to sit a spell right here. *Ah*, there is nothing like resting my
bones after working a full day. I lift my hands and run the fingers of one
hand over the other. It is so lovely to feel sensation keenly—I missed this
world's sharpness.

Let me see you—you will have to come close. Your eyes are so bright,
your skin so flush, your breath so warm, your caress so enticing. Will
you come closer still? If you desire? I want to take you within me, deeper
than I could before, and hold you here for a bit, and let myself sweat and

strain as I pulse around you. And now we press on toward release, not to achieve, but rather to savor, for this night is just one more in a long life to explore.

Let us rest here while I feel you with new fingertips on hands beginning to wrinkle, as I trace your eyelids and brows. You waited for me, like you promised. Am I so changed? Or do I still carry the lines and new grays, the curves and weight? You look just as you did. I am so glad I did not forget your face.

What now? Well, I was thinking... I would love nothing more than to stay here, wrap myself around you, and listen to your stories, if you would enjoy the telling.

Who were you, *before*?

(I have never forgotten your voice.)

I Wrote This Book in Lieu of Dying

The work begun in this orgin story will continue in

A Book of Hours for the End of Time